Pour Me Another
An Opinionated Guide to Gold Country Wines
2011

Volume 1
Amador & El Dorado Counties

Pour Me Another
An Opinionated Guide to Gold Country Wines
2011

Volume 1
Amador and El Dorado Counties

By
David S. Locicero

OpinionatedWineGuide.com
Emeryville, CA

Don't Drink and Drive. Seriously.

The author has taken every effort to ensure that the information in this book was correct at the time the book was printed. But stuff happens and anything and everything is subject to change without notice. The author cannot accept responsibility for any loss, damage, injury or inconvenience from outdated information, errors or omissions. If it is important to you, especially if you are going out of your way to visit, call ahead and confirm. Check local road and weather conditions.

Do Not Drink and Drive.
Seriously.

Published in the United States of America by OpinionatedWineGuide.com. Printed by CreateSpace.com

This book is available at special rates for bulk purchases for sales promotions and premiums. For more information write to the author at 2340 Powell Street, No. 290, Emeryville, CA 94608, or email at info@OpinionatedWineGuide.com .

ISBN: 0615467830

EIN-13: 978-0615467832

For Jeff

Table of Contents

An Opinionated Guide to Gold Country Wines

Introduction

About 6 years ago some very good friends invited us to join them for a wine tasting trip in El Dorado County. This was the first time I had been made aware of wines in California Gold Country.

I was completely enchanted by my first trip the California Gold Country. The landscape was stunning and varied, with rugged hills and lush valleys, agricultural land and forests. And the wines were remarkable. The reds in particular grabbed my pallet and wouldn't let go.

Not only did the wines suit my pallet and my cooking style, but the owners, vintners and proprietors were friendly and enthusiastic about their wines. If you liked one winery's wines, they'd suggest another winery that you also might like. There seemed to be a real community of folks who respected one another and enjoyed sending visitors to their compatriots.

Wine has always been a part of my life. I grew up in a home where there was always a five gallon bottle of something fermenting in the cabinet under the bathroom sink. Well, the bottles weren't originally bubbling away in the bathroom, my father moved there after the time the fermentation pressures built up and caused an explosion in the kitchen, spewing purple liquid all over the room. It was cruel experience that taught my father that someplace easier to clean and less dangerous to the family would be a better location for his wine making experiments.

I recall the first time my father started making wine. I was 8 years old and we were living in a grand old house in the University District in Seattle. He got it in mind to make Mead, a honey based wine. It was an experiment. I remember the gallon jugs with a cloudy, frothy liquid not unlike the color of urine, making an unholy stink in the basement. When the fermentation was complete, I was allowed a taste, and found it horrible. It was strong stuff, it tasted funny and had a fizzy quality that was not like the carbonated beverages to which I was accustomed.

My father started making wine from wine making kits shortly after we moved to Las Vegas, where he taught at the University. His wine made from grapes was much more successful. My father's Zinfandels were his best efforts and were featured on the family table for many years.

As in many Italian American households, wine was seen as food, and an integral part of the meal. I was served watered wine at an early age, say 12 or so, and graduated to undiluted wine when I was in Junior High School. I don't recall every seeing my father drunk, but wine was often served for dinner on a weekday evening, and always when we were entertaining.

After graduating from university, I moved to the San Francisco Bay Area. It wasn't long after I arrived here that I was drawn into the food and wine culture of the area. I loved exploring the wineries of Napa and Sonoma counties and made a point of seeking out wineries when I traveled up into Monterey county, or south to San Luis Obispo and Santa Barbara.

After "discovering" Sierra Foothill wines, we have been back to El Dorado and Amador counties countless times and have tasted wines from nearly every winery in both counties. We have dragged our friends up to Gold Country for wine tasting and are pleased to have turned several of our friends into Gold Country wine boosters as well. Our wine cellar is a monument to Gold Country wines.

The wines in the Sierra Foothills, which also happen to be Gold Country, are varied and diverse. I have a preference for a certain kind of wine that is characteristic of the wines in Amador and El Dorado counties.

In our explorations, I have found that certain areas of the Appellation have more wines that I like than others. This preference will be noted in my tasting notes and comments regarding the various wineries included in this book.

Taste is a very subjective thing. So my opinions about a wine may not coincide with yours. You, in fact, may dislike the wines I like and love the ones I loath. Such is the nature of wine. People who drink wine and take wine seriously have OPINIONS and opinions are wonderful things. Everybody has an opinion. And it will be my opinions that reign supreme in this book. However, every winery description includes a page where you can jot down your own tasting notes and mark down if you agree or disagree with me.

There are well over 100 wineries in Amador and El Dorado counties. I have not yet sampled all the wines from all the wineries. And wineries come and go, especially in this economy, so wineries I once liked have gone out of business and new ones have come into being. The situation is, as they say, fluid.

Consequently, for this book I have chosen to concentrate on those wineries and vineyards that are members of their local wine making associations. The associations are the El Dorado Winery Association (ElDoradoWines.org) and the Amador County Vintners Association (AmadorWine.com).

There is an entry for each member winery. Some entries are longer than others. The longer entries are for wineries that I happen to like for one reason or another. In order to keep this guide to a size something less than a brick, I have had to limit the entries. This does not mean that the wineries with shorter entries are in any way undeserving of a visit or a reflection on their wines. If you are in the area, I encourage you to visit as many of the wineries as you have the time and inclination.

I encourage you to venture into the Gold Country and visit the wineries in this guide. Most of the wines are only available from the wineries, through their respective wine clubs or in a few restaurants in Northern California. Your only opportunity to taste most of these wines is to travel to the Gold Country, seek out the wineries and taste. You won't be sorry.

Don't Drink and Drive. Your life is important.

I have taken every effort to ensure that the information in this book was correct at the time the book was printed. But stuff happens and anything and everything is subject to change without notice. If it is important to you, especially if you are going out of your way to visit, call ahead and confirm. Check the local road and weather conditions and **Don't Drink and Drive.** Seriously.

If in your travels and tastings you find that you agree or disagree with me, let me know! I'd love to hear from you. And if you are familiar with a winery that I have left out and think I should give it a visit, drop me a line. I'm always looking out for a new winery.

David Locicero
David@OpinionatedWineGuide.com

An Opinionated Guide to Gold Country Wines

Acknowledgements

Many people have contributed to this volume. First and foremost, a heartfelt thank you to Virginia McNeil and Jason Crouch, our very good friends, who first introduced us to the wines of El Dorado County, our first foray into the wines of the California Gold Country.

A raised glass of gratitude and a thank you also to Robert, Melicent, Markus, Gladys, Michael and Edward our enthusiastic partners in the exploration of the wineries and wines. I would also like to thank Aisling D'Art for her enthusiasm, support and great ideas for incorporating QR code technology.

Thank you also to the owners, wine makers and tasting room staffs at all of the wineries mentioned in this book.

An Opinionated Guide to Gold Country Wines

Were it not for their skills, talents, friendliness and sense of community, this book never would have come to be.

I would also be remiss if I were not to acknowledge and thank the folks at the El Dorado Winery Association and the Amador County Vintners Association for their awesome websites.

And finally, thank you to my partner in exploration and tasting as well as in life, Jeff Elardo, for his enthusiastic encouragement and adventurous spirit.

The success of this book is in their hands as well as mine, though any and all faults are mine alone.

How to Use This Guide

Guide books are, of necessity, "hands on" type books. They need to be easy to navigate, clear and, in my opinion, provide space for the reader to make their own notes. This guide is designed for the traveler, and is intended to tempt you out to the Gold Country, to help you plan your driving, and to keep track of the wines you tasted and liked.

Organization
This book is divided in to five main sections:
- About Wine Tasting
- Getting to Gold Country
- Gold Country
- Amador County,
- El Dorado County,

An Opinionated Guide to Gold Country Wines

The final two sections make up the heart of the book, with maps and entries for the wineries and vineyards.

Each of the final two sections starts with a map of the specific geographic area with the wineries located in a general way. The map is followed by a brief introduction to the geographic area. Additional, more detailed maps are provided in each geographic section.

I have arranged the wineries in smaller geographical groupings by clusters of wineries to make planning driving easier. Within those smaller groupings the wineries and vineyards are listed in alphabetical order, with each entry having the specific information about the wineries locations, hours of operation, contact information and a description of what I like about the wines.

Please note, most of the wineries are open on Saturday and Sunday. Some are also open on Friday and Monday. A smaller group is open every day. Most will be closed on some national holidays, though not all. Please call ahead if you will be wine tasting on a holiday weekend.

A complete index of wineries and vineyards is provided at the end of the book, with a page reference to the listing.

QR Codes

Each of my maps is accompanied by a QR code, that funny square pattern of black and white boxes. These codes can be read using the camera on your smart phone if you have a bar code scanner app on your phone. When you scan these codes with your bar code scanner app you will be taken to a Google Maps version of the map in your phone.

I have also used the QR codes to provide in-book links to websites for hotels, wineries and so on. I hope that you find this useful!

The QR code above, when scanned with your smart phone's bar code scanner app, will provide a direct link to the companion website, OpinionatedWineGuide.com.

Tasting Notes

In my years of driving these roads and tasting these wines, I have learned that my memory is not as good as it once was. Was that amazing Zinfandel a 2004 or a 2007? Which wine was it that we really loved at Crystal Basin? Where did we buy the futures?

To help you keep track of your wine tasting in Gold Country, this book provides a page for each winery where

An Opinionated Guide to Gold Country Wines

you can note the wines you tasted, what you thought of it and any other information. In this way, I hope to make this guide more useful to you.

Companion Website

This book also has a companion website, OpinionatedWineGuide.com. Books are static, but wine isn't.

Since wine changes as it ages, wineries produce new wines, and new wineries open almost every year, the website allows me to keep you up to date on all of the post publication information and opinions between editions of the guide.

So lets taste!

About Wine Tasting

There is a lot of fuss and bother about wine tasting. The activity is rife with language that most people don't use. It is portrayed with a seemingly endless list of esoteric nonsense that makes wine tasting seem out of reach of the ordinary wine drinker at best, or pretentious twaddle at worst.

I believe that wine tasting is really a very simple activity that can be as nuanced or as straight forward as you are comfortable with. In this section, I'll touch on some basics of wine tasting to give you, if you have never partaken in the activity before, an idea of what to expect and what is expected of you. I'll also provide you with an introduction to wine tasting that both beginners and seasoned drinkers can put to use.

I encourage you to take notes as you are tasting wines. It sounds wine-geeky, but if you start taking notes, it helps you to slow down in your tasting and be more deliberate about it. Also, if you are tasting and drinking wine on a regular basis, keeping tasting notes will help you remember the wines you've had, whether you liked them or not and if you might want to buy it when facing a familiar label in the store.

In this book each winery description has a page for taking tasting notes. It is my hope that by recording your impressions of the wines, the book will become a lasting reference for your travels through Gold Country and your explorations of Gold Country wines.

Tasting Room Etiquette

If this is your first time to go wine tasting, you are in for a treat. Most wineries, and all of the wineries and vineyards in this book, have a tasting room, a room that is open to the public where they pour samples of wines for you to taste. Their hope is that you will like one or more of the wines well enough to make a purchase.

If you've been to Napa or Sonoma counties recently, you've seen the ridiculous amounts of money they are charging for wine tastings. There is often a fee associated with tasting, usually between $10 and $45 per person. In Amador and El Dorado counties, only a very few wineries have tasting fees. And the fees in Gold Country are usually between $3 and $5. This is one of the many reasons I prefer Gold Country wineries to those in Napa and Sonoma Counties. And pretty much any winery where they do charge for tastings, will waive all or a portion of the fee if you do make a purchase.

There once was a time when wineries might offer you a souvenir wine glass when you paid for a tasting. Those days are long gone. A few places in Napa and Sonoma still do this, but don't expect it here in Gold Country. You're here to taste wine, not amass a collection of glasses.

Normally, you will be offered white wines first and then work your way through the offerings from the lightest wines through to the most robust and flavorful. It is okay to say, "I'm only drinking reds today", or "I'd like to skip the port". Especially if you are driving, you probably will want to sample only one or two wines at any one place.

The standard pour for tasting is about half an ounce. It isn't much. But it is enough to get a good idea of the wine's aroma and the flavor. In most cases, after you've tasted a couple of wines, it's okay to ask for a second pour of a previous wine.

Often times you won't like the wine so much, or the pour will have been more than you really needed to get a sense of the wine. Every winery will have a bucket or container of some sort on the bar where you can pour out the wine. You're under no obligation to drink every drop of every pour. In fact, if you're going to visit more than one or two wineries in a day, you'll probably not want to do that. It is completely fine to dump out the excess pour. The wineries will also provide pitchers of water so you can rinse the glass or even rinse your palate.

Unlike European tasting rooms, spitting out the wine after you've tasted it is NOT done here. So don't look for a spittoon!

Look at the Wine

Once the friendly person behind the bar has poured your taste, before you do anything, look at the wine. Note the color. Can you see through the wine? Does light penetrate through the wine at all? You would be surprised how dark some red wines can be.

Smell the Wine

Once you have taken note of the color, give the wine glass a good swirl, clockwise or counter clockwise. If you are new to this, keep the glass on the bar and just move the base of the glass around in a tight circle, enough to get the wine swirling around in the glass.

The reason you do this is to get some oxygen into the wine. Doing so helps to release the aromas in the wine and will "open up" the aromas and flavors, making them more pronounced. This is similar to letting a wine breath before serving.

Once you've swirled the wine, pick up the glass and put your nose right into the glass and give it a good sniff. The practical reason to do this is to see if the wine has gone to vinegar. Since you're in a tasting room, that is very unlikely. The main reason to do this is to smell the wine, get to know it. The aroma of a wine is called its "nose". So when some wine snob is going on and on about the "nose" of this or that wine, that's all it is, the aroma or smell of the wine.

It is a little know Wine Fact that 8 times out of 10 what you will smell when you put your nose in the glass is wine. That is a shocker, I know! In my experience, when you're starting out the wine for which you can be specific about the constituent aromas, say, "ah, I smell honeysuckle and vanilla" is not all that common. That percentage will improve the more times you've smelled wine.

I've been doing this for a long time so I'd say that roughly 7 times out of 10 I can say, "this has an herbal aroma with earthy undertones" and not be speaking complete bollocks. But this is a major part of tasting and is a skill that does improve over time. So stick your nose in there and inhale deeply. You may surprise yourself at what you can smell.

The person at the counter may suggest that you might get hints of this fruit or that flower. As you smell the wine, see if you can smell those. But if you can't, don't worry about it.

Taste the Wine

Now, take a sip. Don't chug the whole thing, but just take a sip and swish it around in your mouth, or even make a chewing motion. The point of this exercise is to get the wine in your mouth into contact with all the taste buds on your tongue.

We taste different basic flavor characteristics – salt, sweet, bitter, sour and savory - on different parts of our tongues. So by moving the wine around in our mouths on the first sip or two we are able to ensure that we really taste everything the wine has to offer.

Another little known Wine Fact is that when you sip on a wine you will taste wine. Similar to the smell of a wine, tasting the constituent flavors of the wine is a skill that comes with time. Generally, for most wines, you will be able to say that you can taste a little cherry, currants, raisins, stone fruit, citrus or what have you. The more wines you taste and the more you pair wines with foods, the better at it you will become.

Again, the friendly person who poured your taste will often suggest that you will taste hints of several things. You may, or you may not.

With California wines you are likely to get either a big blast of fruit on the first taste or an overwhelming sense of dryness. The puckering dryness is caused by tannins. Some people like that, I don't, but very often a wine will become less tannic with age.

A good balance of fruit and tannin is referred to as "structure". If a wine has a good "structure", it usually means that the wine can be held for a longer time in your cellar to be consumed in 5 or 10 or more years.

An Opinionated Guide to Gold Country Wines

Occasionally, if the wine has been kept in barrels for more than a year or so, you may also get a flavor akin to sucking on a piece of wood. This is what is known as "oak". The wooden barrels used to age wines are made out of oak. Some wineries will brag about their French Oak barrels. Other will say they switch their wines from American Oak barrels to French Oak barrels. It does impact the flavor of the wine, particularly white wines, like Chardonnay.

In most cases this oak flavor adds to the flavor profile of the wine. Though occasionally, it will have been over done. I recently had a Cabernet Sauvignon that had spent 2 years in oak barrels and, one sip and I thought I might have to pull the splinters out of my tongue. I had never had such an oaky wine.

And this is where wine tasting is so fun. The flavor of a wine will change over time. It will change from the time it is in the barrel to the time it gets bottled. A 2010 wine will taste different in 2011 than it will in 2013 and it will continue to change as it ages and you taste it again in 2018 or 2022.

And the wine will taste different when you first open the bottle than it will an hour later. Sometimes the wine will improve the longer it has been open, other times it will lose something over time. The changes may be subtle or extreme. There is really no way of knowing. And that is what is so endlessly fascinating about wine tasting.

Developing Your Palate

As you drink wine you will find that you like some wines and don't like others. Everybody's palate is different. I happen to like robust reds, like Zinfandels and Bordeaux blends. Others like lighter reds like Sangiovese or Merlots.

The longer you taste wines and the more different kinds of wines you taste, the more you will both get to know your palate and the more educated your palate will become. Taking tasting notes will help you develop your palate as it is an excellent memory prompt.

Twenty years ago, I laughed at those people who were sniffing wines and yammering on about the constituent flavors of wines. I thought they were a bunch of pretentious idiots.

Well, I was half right. They were being pretentious. But they weren't idiots. I have learned the skills they knew and have entered their realm. You can, too. My palate has been educated and I know what I like. The more we taste, the more we can taste with every wine. It's fun.

We can taste and enjoy wine long before we have the skills. Our palates are very sensitive and though our brains may not have been trained yet, you can generally tell a good wine from a bad wine long before your palate has developed. Don't be intimidated by wine snobs. Drink wines you like. Sample new wines regularly. The whole point is enjoying the wines.

An Opinionated Guide to Gold Country Wines

Since our palates are individual things and we have different wine tasting experience and cook in different ways, there is no necessary relationship between price and quality when it comes to wine. We have all had great cheap wines and awful expensive wines. So drink what you like!

Getting to Gold Country

The California Gold Country is only a two to two and half hour drive from San Francisco and two and a half hour drive from Reno. You can make it a nice day trip from the San Francisco Bay Are or Reno, though it will be a long-ish day.

If you leave the Bay Area between 8:30 and 9:00 AM, you can be sipping wine at Gold Hill, David Girard or Sera Fina by 10:30 or 11:00.

The majority of wineries in Amador County are grouped together in two areas. The wineries in El Dorado County are similarly grouped in three areas. It is possible to visit 4 to 7 wineries, including breaking for a picnic lunch before heading back to the Bay Area. A similar trip is possible from Reno.

An Opinionated Guide to Gold Country Wines

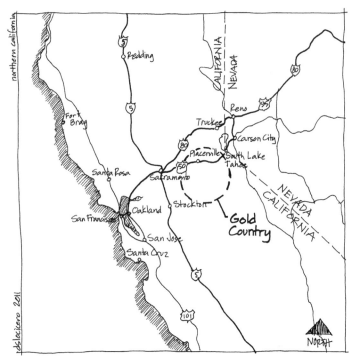

Map of Northern California

I have made numerous day trips from the Bay Area to Amador and El Dorado counties over the years. It is a nice escape. My favorite way to visit the Gold Country is to make it an over-night or weekend trip. I will leave the Bay Area around 9:00 AM. Then I will check into the hotel in El Dorado Hills, my preferred base of operations. This way I can spend the better part of two days tasting wine before heading back late the second day.

Driving in Gold Country

Once you get off Highway 50 the roads in Gold Country are mostly two lanes and travel through agricultural land and small towns and hamlets. The speed limits will vary between 25 mph and 65 mph, depending on the situation. Be respectful of the residents and adhere to the speed limits.

The signage can be problematic. Some of the maps in this book also have a QR Code which, when scanned with the bar code scanner on your smart phone, will take you directly to the Google Maps map of the area. It is my hope that this will make it easier for you to navigate the roads without getting lost.

When I drive up from the Bay Area, I generally stop for gas in either Folsom or in El Dorado Hills and top off the gas tank. With my car, this means I will be able to drive from winery to winery and still have enough gas to get home without stopping for gas again. If you're coming in from Reno or South Lake Tahoe, you may want to stop for gas in Placerville.

From The Bay Area

The drive from the Bay Area is easy. If you are on the Peninsula or in San Francisco, simply get on 101 headed North and East, cross the Bay Bridge and get onto highway 80 to Sacramento.

If you are in the East bay, get onto 880 headed North and East connecting to 80 going in the same direction. Follow 80 through Hercules, Vallejo, Fairfield and Davis.

An Opinionated Guide to Gold Country Wines

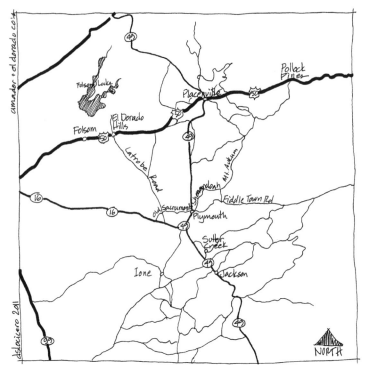

Map of Gold Country.

Scan QR code for Google Map of Gold Country

In Sacramento, the highway splits and you will want to follow the signs for Highway 50, toward Placerville and South Lake Tahoe.

Most of the wineries in El Dorado County are easily accessible off of Highway 50. (See map, page 36.)

The wineries in Amador County are further south. If you are coming up from the Bay Area, the quickest way to get there is to exit Highway 50 at Latrobe Road. At the bottom of the ramp, turn right onto Latrobe Road. You will have no choice. Follow Latrobe South.

At Old Sacramento Road, you will have a decision to make:

- If you continue on Latrobe Road you will be headed toward one of the two major groupings of wineries. These wineries are less closely clustered, but you will be able to visit the old Gold Rush towns of Drytown and Sutter Creek, both of which are delightful destinations of their own.
- If you turn Left onto Old Sacramento Road you will be headed toward the other of the two major groupings of wineries. There are more wineries in this group and they are more closely grouped.

(See map, page 38.)

From Reno

If you are driving in from Reno or South Lake Tahoe, you want to take Highway 80 West. Follow 80 west until Auburn, California. In Auburn, take the exit onto

An Opinionated Guide to Gold Country Wines

Highway 49 South and follow it to Placerville and Highway 50.

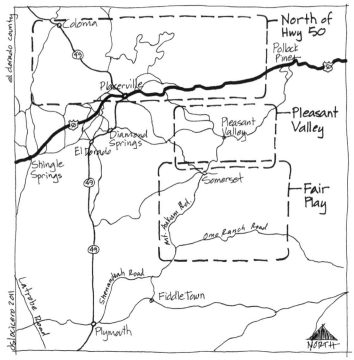

Map of El Dorado County showing groupings of wineries.

Scan QR code for El Dorado Winery Association map of wineries

From Placerville, you can either get onto Highway 50 to visit the El Dorado County wineries, (see map, page 34) or stay on 49 and head down to Plymouth.

In Plymouth, you have a choice of turning left onto Shenandoah Road, which will take you to the larger of the two Amador County groups of wineries. Or you can continue South on 49 toward Drytown and Sutter Creek. Honestly, if you're thirsty, the added 30 minutes may make the left turn onto Shenandoah Road more attractive to you. (See map, page 36.)

From South Lake Tahoe

If you are driving in from South Lake Tahoe, you want to take Highway 50 West. This will take you directly into Placerville. The El Dorado County wineries are easily accessible from Highway 50. (See map, page 34.)

To get to the Amador County wineries, in Placerville, take Highway 49 South toward Plymouth.

In Plymouth, you have a choice of turning left onto Shenandoah Road, which will take you to the larger of the two Amador County groups of wineries. Or you can continue South on 49 toward Drytown and Sutter Creek. Honestly, if you're thirsty, the added 30 minutes may make the left turn onto Shenandoah Road more attractive to you. (See map, page 36.)

Wine Tours

If you are traveling from Sacramento, South Lake Tahoe and Reno, there are commercial wine tours available from

An Opinionated Guide to Gold Country Wines

Map of Amador County showing groupings of wineries.

Scan the QR code for the Amador Vintners Association map of member wineries.

each city that will take you for a nice day trip. You won't have to drive, freeing you up to taste a few more wines, though space is often limited on these tours, so your purchases may be limited to a bottle or two here and there. Check the local yellow pages or with your hotel concierge for information about these commercial wine tours.

If you are making your own wine tour with a rented limo, call ahead to the wineries to ensure that they will be able to accommodate you. Some of the wineries have narrow winding approaches which make limousines problematic.

An Opinionated Guide to Gold Country Wines

Where to Stay / Where to Eat

While it is possible to make your trip to the Gold Country a day trip from either the Bay Area or from Reno, my favorite way to visit the area is as an overnight or weekend trip.

Lodging

I have stayed at several different places when I have traveled up to the Gold Country. Hands down, my favorite place to stay is the Holiday Inn Express in El Dorado Hills.

El Dorado Hills is a suburb of Sacramento, nestled up into the foothills. The main exit is at Latrobe Road. The Holiday Inn Express is located at the El Dorado Hills Town Center, a development on the left of Latrobe Road, just as you exit Highway 50.

An Opinionated Guide to Gold Country Wines

I like staying here for several reasons. First, the hotel is new, clean, and expertly run. The staff is wonderful, friendly and knowledgeable. I had only stayed there two or three times and the staff recognized my partner and I when we arrived. This made us really feel at home.

Second, the El Dorado Hills Town Center is like a small upscale village. Once you've parked at the hotel you can walk to coffee, walk to dinner, walk to the movie theater. It really is convenient. After spending all day driving from winery to winery, it is just nice to be able to stroll out of the hotel and to a restaurant for dinner.

I am not the only one who likes staying at the Holiday Inn Express in El Dorado Hills. They are frequently booked up. When that happens my second choice is to stay at the Courtyard by Marriott in Folsom. The Courtyard by Marriott is located one mile east of Latrobe Road at the Scott Road Exit. They are visible from the Highway, and located on Iron Point Road.

While there are many restaurants in the area of the Courtyard by Marriott, it is difficult to walk to them and they are mostly, though not entirely, fast food restaurants.

I have also stayed in Placerville at the historic Cary House Hotel. The Cary House has much to recommend it: it is located in the center of Placerville, which is a great Gold Rush town, within walking distance of several good restaurants and great shopping, and centrally located for access to the wineries. If you want to stay in an historic hotel, said to be haunted, it is an option.

There are other hotels in the area, and there are a multitude of Bed and Breakfasts in the area as well. If you prefer to stay at a B&B, you may be spoiled for choice. There are many in both Amador and El Dorado counties. I have not stayed at any of the B&B's included here. Each of the listed B&B's was recommended to me by people I trust. But please use your own judgment before making any reservations.

You can also stay at the Fitzpatrick Winery and Lodge in Fair Play, south of Placerville, in the heart of the Fair Play region and convenient to the Amador County wineries. A friend of mine, stayed at the Fitzpatrick Winery and Lodge and loved it. The winery and lodge is located atop a hill with a spectacular view of the Fair Play area and the snowcapped Sierra's. While it is more remote than other options, it will give you a real taste of wine country living.

Hotels
Holiday Inn Express
> 4360 Town Center Blvd
> El Dorado Hills, CA 95762
> Phone: 916-358-3100
> www.hiexpress.com/hotels/us/en/el-dorado-hills/edhls/hoteldetail

An Opinionated Guide to Gold Country Wines

Courtyard by Marriott
   2575 Iron Point Road
   Folsom, California 95630
   Phone: 916-984-7624
   www.marriott.com/hotels/travel/sacfo-courtyard-sacramento-folsom

Cary House Hotel
   300 Main Street
   Placerville, CA 95667
   Phone: 530-622-4271
   www.caryhouse.com

Bed and Breakfasts

Albert Shafsky House
    2942 Colma Street
    Placerville, CA 95667
    Phone: 530-642-2776
    Email: stay@shafsky.com
    www.shafsky.com

Eden Vale Inn Bread & Breakfast
    1780 Springvale Road
    Placerville, CA 95667
    Phone: 530-621-0901
    Email: innkeeper@edenvaleinn.com
    www.edenvaleinn.com

An Opinionated Guide to Gold Country Wines

Bella Vista Bed & Breakfast
  581 Cold Springs Rd.
  Placerville, CA 95667
  Phone: 530-622-3456
  Email:Kathleen@discoverbellavista.com
  www.discoverbellavista.com

Sutter Creek Inn
  75 Main Street, P.O. Box 385
  Sutter Creek, CA 95685
  Phone: 209-267-5606
  Email: info@suttercreekinn.com
  www.suttercreekinn.com

Plymouth House Inn
      9525 Main Street
      Plymouth, CA 95669
      Phone: 209-245-3298
      Email: plymouthhouseinn@att.net
      www.plymouthhouseinn.com

Amador City Hotel, Saloon & Restaurant
      14202 Old Highway 49
      Amador City, CA 95601
      Phone: 209-267-9172
      Email: info@imperialamador.com
      www.imperialamador.com

Fitzpatrick Winery and Lodge
      7740 Fair Play Road
      Fair Play, CA 95864
      Phone: 800-245-9166
      www.fitzpatrickwinery.com

Food

To be honest, where to eat in the area is a bigger problem than where to stay or where to drink. In El Dorado Hills, Placerville or Sutter Creek, there are places to eat. But if you are out on the road, it is rural and there aren't a ton of places to stop for a quick meal, a sandwich or picnic fixings. I usually plan on eating a picnic lunch and pack a small cooler with my own picnic foods. Then we'll stop at one of the wineries that welcomes picnickers. For dinner, we'll eat at one of our favorite places in El Dorado Hills.

In **El Dorado Hills**, I recommend three restaurants, in no particular order:

Bistro 33

Wonderful California Cuisine. They carry local wines.
4364 Town Center Blvd.
El Dorado Hills, CA 95762
Phone: 916-358-3733
edh.bistro33.com

Bamiyan Afghan Restaurant

This is really a great place for Afghan food! They carry local wines.
1121 White Rock Rd.
El Dorado Hills, CA 95762
Phone: 916-941-8787
www.afghancuisine.com

An Opinionated Guide to Gold Country Wines

Chantara Thai Cuisine
> After a day drinking wine, sometimes a nice Thai meal and some beer is just the thing.
> 4361 Town Center Blvd.
> El Dorado Hills, CA 95762
> 916-939-0389
> Chantarathaicuisine.com

In **Placerville**, I recommend three restaurants:

Z Pie
> Wonderful selection of individual pot pies.
> 3182 Center Street
> Placerville, CA 95667
> Phone: 530-621-2626
> www.z-pie.com

Heyday Café
>
> Really good for breakfast or lunch.
> 325 Main Street
> Placerville, CA 95667
> Phone: 530-626-9700
> www.heydaycafe.com

Cascada
>
> After a day of wine tasting, unwind here.
> 384 Main Street
> Placerville, CA 95667
> Phone: 530-344-7757
> www.cascadaonmainstreet.com

An Opinionated Guide to Gold Country Wines

In **Somerset** I recommend:

Gold Vine Grill
> This place is pretty swishy and a tad pricey, but good.
> 6028 Grizzly Flat Rd.
> Somerset, CA 95684
> Phone: 530-626-4042
> www.goldvinegrill.com

Crossroads Coffee & Café
> Great sandwiches. Family run.
> 6032 Grizzly Flat Rd.
> Somerset, CA 95684
> Phone: 530-344-0591
> www.facebook.com/pages/Crossroads-Coffee-Cafe/144024222315594?sk=info

Finally, in **Sutter Creek**, these are my recommendations.

Thomi's Coffee & Eatery
I LOVE Thomi. She is the best. We always eat here
when we're in Sutter Creek.
40-C Hanford Street
Sutter Creek, CA 95685
Phone: 209-267-1108
Suttercreek.org/dine/thomis-coffee-eatery

Susan's Place Wine Bar & Eatery
15 Eureka Street
Sutter Creek, CA 95685
Phone: 209-267-0945
www.susansplace.com

An Opinionated Guide to Gold Country Wines

And I would be remiss not to mention, in **El Dorado**:

Poor Red's Bar-B-Q
      6221 Pleasant Valley Rd.
      El Dorado, Ca 95623
      Phone: 530-622-2901
      www.poorredsbbq.com

There are other places to eat in the area. If you find a great place not mentioned here, please drop me a line and let me know about it: info@opinionatedwineguide.com.

Gold Country

When I tell people in the Bay Area that I write about Gold Country Wines, almost everyone thinks that I write about Napa and Sonoma counties. Clearly the term "Gold Country" is not a meaningful signifier for many Californians.

I'll respond, "No, Sierra Foothills wines." This elicits blank looks. "Placerville," I'll say, "on the way to South Lake Tahoe."

At this point a look of astonishment will cross their faces and they will ask with incredulity, "There are wineries up there?"

Yes. Yes there are. There are over 100 in Amador and El Dorado counties alone. The wines are good in Gold

An Opinionated Guide to Gold Country Wines

Country. Many Napa, Sonoma and Central Coast wineries buy their Zinfandel grapes from Amador and El Dorado county vineyards.

Not every winery is a winner, but that can also be said of any other wine making region in California. But there are enough good ones, and a few really great ones, to make the drive worthwhile.

In addition to the great wine, there are also some really charming and friendly Gold Rush towns. Placerville, the El Dorado County Seat, is also known as "Hang Town" because of the reputation of a late 19th century judge for

View down the main street of Sutter Creek.

hanging those convicted of crimes. Those days are done. Now the town is a lively center for life in the county with interesting shopping and good restaurants.

In Amador County, I really like Sutter Creek. It is smaller than Placerville. It has retained its old Gold Rush era wooden Victorian buildings and feels very "old west". The shopping may not be as extensive as in Placerville, but the town has a great history, fun antiquing and some great places to eat.

This book is focused on the wines produced in Gold Country, but there is a lot to see and do in addition to wine tasting. Take some time to drive the back roads. Stop in to the small towns. Check out the small museums and the gold mines. Take some time and go rafting or fly fishing. You won't be sorry!

A Little History
Amador and El Dorado counties, Gold Country as I am calling this area, was the area where gold was first discovered in the middle of the 19th century.

Gold was discovered in 1848 on the South Fork of the American River at Sutter's Mill. The gold attracted people from all over the country and from all over the world. The Gold Rush put this area on the map and determined the character of the region that still exists.

The Spanish missionaries who travelled up California establishing the chain of Missions along the El Camino Real brought grape plants with them for the production of

An Opinionated Guide to Gold Country Wines

sacramental wine. It wasn't until after the start of the Gold Rush and the massive influx of miners and prospectors to the region that a market for wine, to quench the thirst of all the rowdy miners, that grapes were planted in any significant numbers.

In the 1850's and 1860's vineyards were planted for commercial wine production. In addition to cuttings from the Mission grapes, cuttings were brought in from the east coast of the United States, including the now dominant Zinfandel varietal. Italian miners, realizing the similarities between their native Mediterranean climate and the Gold Country climate sought out and planted Italian grape varietals.

For a short time this was the location of the first commercial winery in the United States, established in El Dorado County by James Skinner in the 1850's. By the 1870's El Dorado County was the third largest wine producing area after Los Angeles and Sonoma counties.

After the turn of the century, wine making started to decline in the area and the passage of prohibition put an end to most commercial wine making. Some families continued to make sacramental wine for church use, as well as making wines for personal consumption. Vineyard were torn up and replaced with orchards.

It wasn't until the late 1960's and early 1970's that grape growing and wine making returned to the area. In 1973 Boeger was one of the very first vineyards and wineries to open up commercial production after prohibition.

AVA

There are about 200 American Viticultural Areas, refered to as AVA's, in the United States. This is the system of wine appellations of origin used in the United States. AVA's are recognized wine growing regions which are based on geographic, climate and soil characteristics. AVA's can be and are subdivided into smaller AVA's.

The boundaries of AVA's are defined by the Alcohol and tobacco Tax and Trade Bureau, an office within the United States Department of the Treasury.

In most Europe an appellation designation not only limits the grapes to those grown within the geographical area, but also what grape varietals can be used within the wine, methods of growing and crop yields. American AVA's are more like the Italian system, which only requires that 85% of the grapes used to make the wine be grown within the appellation.

The main AVA in Gold country is the Sierra Foothills AVA. This AVA includes all of Amador, Calaveras, El Dorado, Nevada and Placer counties. If a wine has "Sierra Foothills" on the label, 85% of the grapes used to make the wine must have been grown in these 5 counties.

Amador County and El Dorado County are each Sub AVA's of the Sierra Foothills AVA. When a label has the name of one of these counties on its label, at least 85% of the grapes used to make the wine must have been grown in the named county.

An Opinionated Guide to Gold Country Wines

Confused yet?

To add to the confusion, sub-AVA's can be and are further subdivided into even smaller AVA's based distinct, recognized variations in the geography, climate and soils. The El Dorado AVA contains the smaller Fair Play AVA. The same 85% rule applies to wines that say "Fair Play" on the label.

Estate and Reserve Wines

In addition to the AVA designations, wineries will also use terms like "Estate" and "Reserve" to refer to wines. There is no statutory definition for these terms, so meanings may vary a bit from winery to winery.

"Estate" wines, in general, are made from grapes grown in the vineyards of the wine maker, and not from grapes grown by others. You would think that wine makers who buy all their grapes obviously could not produce an "Estate" wine. But they can. If they make a wine only from grapes from one vineyard, they have in effect produced an "Estate" wine. Most will not label it as an Estate wine, but will identify the vineyard on the label.

So called "Reserve" wines have two different possible meanings. In both cases, the fruit is assumed to be the best the wine maker could find for that specific wine. One meaning is that the vintner has held back these grapes for his or her own wine making, and sold the rest of the crop to other wine makers. The other way "Reserve" is used is similar in that the wine maker has gone through the vineyard and hand selected the grapes he wants to use in this specific wine reserving the fruit with the desired characteristics for that wine. The rest of the fruit was either used in less other, less premium wines.

Grape Varietals

The list of grapes grown in Gold Country is really long. Because of the climate, soils and elevation, a wide range of grapes from many different wine making regions can be grown here. This provides the wine makers with many options for not only what to grow, but what styles of wines to make.

Making a broad generalization, the difference between European wine making and American, especially California wine making, is this: European wines are about the region and the *terroir* – a French word that has no direct English equivalent, but roughly means "the character of the land and climate as it manifests itself in the wine" – whereas American wines are more about the fruit.

There are, of course exceptions, so don't send me hate mail. But as a generality, it stands, I think. The French system of appellations dictates not only what grapes can be used in a wine, but what wine making techniques can be used.

When you speak of a Bordeaux or a Burgundy or a Rhone wine, those are names of wine making appellations. Many different grapes are grown in those regions and there is a great likelihood that the wine you are drinking is a blend of two or more grapes.

An Opinionated Guide to Gold Country Wines

In California, we are more likely to discuss the specific grape varietal: Cabernet Sauvignon, Chardonnay, Merlot, and so on. While there are wine makers making blends here, American's seem to have a much more grape-centric approach to wines. We want to know what specific grapes are in the wine.

The other difference between European and American, and especially California wines, is that domestic wines are much more likely to have a big blast of fruit on the first sip of wine, followed, often by tannins or acid and then a peppery or spicy finish. This makes for a great tasting room experience, but makes it more difficult to pair wines with foods because the wines often lack subtlety and depth.

European wine, on the other hand, doesn't have that fruity first impression. It takes more time to get to know the wines as their flavors open up over and change over the span of an hour or more. These wines are not as dramatic on your palate, but they drink more easily and are able to be paired with more foods than say, BBQ.

These are generalizations, and there are 100's of wines which will prove me wrong, but 1000's of wines that will support me. I'm not saying that one style or another is better than the other. I'm just saying there are differences. I like wines made in both styles, and you will note them in my descriptions throughout the book.

But I digress.

Zinfandel
The king of the grapes in Gold Country is the Zinfandel grape. The grape is genetically related to two European grapes, the Italian Primitivo and the Croatian Crljenak Kastelanski (try saying that 3 times fast!). The clippings were brought here originally from plants on the east coast of the US, via Austria, and later directly from Italy. The plant thrives in our hot days and cool nights with hot summers and relatively mild winters. Nearly every winery in Gold Country makes at least one Zinfandel.

Mission
Mission grapes have been matched genetically to an obscure Spanish grape, Listan Prieto. It is now uncommon in Spain, but is grown in the Canary Islands as Palomino Negro. The grape is a good producer and is adaptable to many different climates, making it the ideal grape for missionaries to carry with them around the world. The grapes were planted throughout California by the Spanish missionaries for making sacramental wines. Only a few Gold Country wineries still grow and make wines from Mission grapes.

The geology, climate and soils in Gold Country primarily are similar to the Rhone and Italian regions, as well as to Bordeaux and Spain. Many of the wineries here specialize in Rhone varietals, Bordeaux varietals or Italian varietals. Most of the grapes in these categories are reasonably well known now, so I will list the major grapes from each of these areas so you'll know what to expect when a winery says they specialize in Rhone wines or whatever.

63

An Opinionated Guide to Gold Country Wines

Bordeaux

The major Bordeaux grapes most commonly grown in Gold Country are:

Reds:

> Cabernet Franc
> Cabernet Sauvignon
> Malbec
> Merlot
> Petite Verdot

Whites:

> Sauvignon Blanc
> Semillion

Rhone

The major Rhone grapes most commonly grown in Gold Country are:

Reds:

> Carignon
> Counoise
> Grenache
> Mourvedre
> Syrah
> Petite Sirah

Whites:

> Grenache Blanc
> Marsanne
> Roussanne
> Viognier

Italian Varietals

The major Italian varietals most commonly grown in Gold Country are:

Reds:

Anglianco
Barbera
Montepulciano
Nebbiolo
Primitivo
Sangiovese

Whites:

Fiano
Malvasia Bianco
Moscato
Pinot Grigio
Vermentino

Spanish Varietals

The major Spanish varietals most commonly grown in Gold Country are:

Reds:

Tempranillo

Whites:

Malvasia
Verdejo (Verdelho)

Other Varietals

There are vineyards growing other grapes from each of these regions as well as grapes from many other wine regions of the world.

Chardonnay

Chardonnay is a grape varietal originally from Burgundy in France. The French version of Chardonnay is called

An Opinionated Guide to Gold Country Wines

Chablis. It is the most common grape used to make French Champagne.

While many Gold Country wineries are making Chardonnay, and it is grown in Gold Country, I personally feel that it is not an ideal grape to grow in Gold Country. It thrives in climates with which are characterized by higher humidity, hot days and cool nights with morning fog. Napa and Sonoma counties are ideal places to grow Chardonnay. In my opinion most of the Gold Country Chardonnay's just are not quite as good as those from Napa and Sonoma.

Amador County

For the purposes of this book, I have divided the wineries into two large groups which I am calling the Sutter Creek group and the Shenandoah Road group.

The Sutter Creek group is made up of wineries south and East of Plymouth. These wineries are spaced further apart. (See map, page 69.)

The Shenandoah Road group, the larger of the two groups, is made up of wineries north and east of Plymouth. The Shenandoah Road Group has three sub groupings: Shenandoah Road (see map, page 71), Shenandoah School Road (see map, page 73) and the Steiner and Bell Roads (see map, page 74).

An Opinionated Guide to Gold Country Wines

Map of Amador County showing groupings of wineries. See page 38 for a QR code that will take you directly to the Amador Vintners Association map of member wineries.

See page 34 for a QR code that will take you directly to a Google Map of the Gold Country.

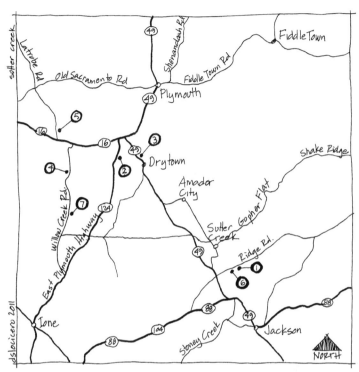

Map of Sutter Creek area wineries.

An Opinionated Guide to Gold Country Wines

In an effort to make your trip planning easier, and help you eliminate doubling back and travelling the same roads forward and back, I have grouped the wineries in geographic areas. Refer to the maps for the most efficient driving. But for ease of reference, the winery descriptions themselves are arranged in the ever popular alphabetical order.

Sutter Creek Wineries

As you are driving around this area, take the time to get off the highway and go into Amador City and on to Sutter Creek. Sutter Creek has several nice places to eat and is the location of the Scott Harvey Wines tasting room. Not discussed in this guide because Scott Harvey is not a member of the Amador Wine Association, his wines are very good and the tasting room is worth a visit.

The Sutter Creek group of wineries (see map, page 69) includes the following:

1 Avio Vineyard & Winery
2 Convergence Vineyards
3 Drytown Cellars
4 Nua Dair
5 Sera Fina
6 Sierra Ridge Vineyards & Winery
7 Tanis

Shenandoah Road Wineries

I have divided the Shenandoah Road wineries into three groups as follows:

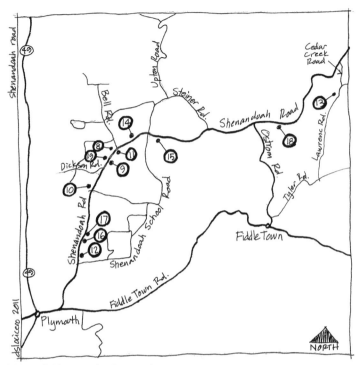

Map of Shenandoah Road wineries.

Shenandoah Road Group
(See map on page 69.)

8 Amador Cellars
9 Andis Wines
10 Bantam Cellars
11 Borjon Winery

An Opinionated Guide to Gold Country Wines

12 Bray Vineyards
13 Il Gioiello Wines & Morse Wines
14 Helwig Vineyards & Winery
15 Karmere Vineyards & Winery
16 Nine Gables Vineyard
17 Jeff Runquist
18 Sobon Estate
19 Vino Noceto

Shenandoah School Road
(See map, page 73)

20 C.G. DiArie Vineyard & Winery
21 Cooper Vineyards
22 Terra D'Oro
23 Wildrotter Vineyard

Steiner and Bell Roads
(See map, page 74)

24 Amador Foothill Winery
25 Charles Spinetta Winery & Wild Life Art Gallery
26 Deaver Vineyards
27 Dillian Wines
28 Dobra Zemlja
29 Driven Cellars
30 Karly
31 Renwood Winery
32 Shenandoah Vineyards
33 Story Winery
34 Terre Rouge & Easton Wines
35 TKC Vineyards

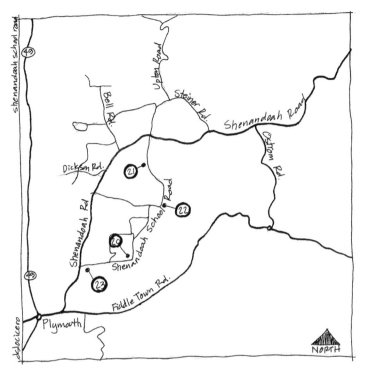

Map of the Shenandoah School Road wineries.

An Opinionated Guide to Gold Country Wines

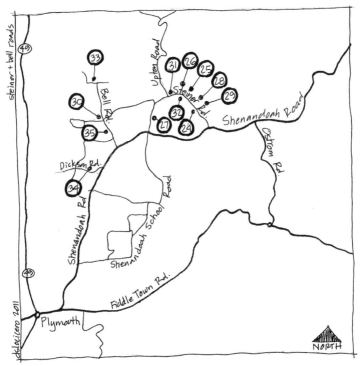

Map of the Steiner and Bell Road wineries.

Sutter Creek Wineries

Avio Vineyards and Winery

Open Friday - Sunday 11am - 5pm and by appt.

14520 Ridge Rd.
Sutter Creek CA 95685
209-267-1515
www.aviowine.com

Avio Vineyards is a relatively new winery, established in the last decade. Coming from an Italian wine making family, the owners are following their wine making heritage in Amador County rather than Italy.

They continue the Tuscan traditions with their Tuscan style farmstead, complete with courtyard and fountain. They avoid mechanization in their 30 acres of sustainably farmed vineyards and do everything by hand. They often host weddings and other special events.

Avio specializes in Italian-style varietals. Their 'Handcrafted Wines' include Aglianico, Barbera, Zinfandel, Sangiovese, and Pinot Grigio. They also produce distinctly un-Italian Merlot and Cabernet Sauvignon. They strive to make wines which are balanced and smooth, unlike many California wines.

Tasting Notes:

Wine: _____Year:_____
Notes:_____
_____
_____
_____

Wine: _____Year:_____
Notes:_____
_____
_____
_____

Wine: _____Year:_____
Notes:_____
_____
_____
_____

Wine: _____Year:_____
Notes:_____
_____
_____
_____

Wine: _____Year:_____
Notes:_____
_____
_____
_____

Convergence Vineyards

Open Friday - Sunday 10am – 5pm and by appointment. Large groups and limos by appointment only - please call ahead.

> 14650 Hwy 124
> Plymouth CA 95669
> 209-245-3600
> www.convergencevineyards.com

Convergence Vineyards is named for a location where the Amador, Rancheria, and Dry creeks converge into a single waterway. The family run winery was established in 2000 by Stephen and Jamie Concannon.

They grow and make wines from Sauvignon Blanc, Viognier, Barbera, Mourvedre, Zinfandel, Syrah and Petite Sirah. They use sustainable farming techniques. Several of their wines are award winners and worth checking out. This is a low production winery, and their wines do sell out.

They also have an educational vineyard planted on the property with different varietals planted using different trellis systems.

Tasting Notes:

Wine: _____Year:_____
Notes:_____

_____
_____
_____

Wine: _____Year:_____
Notes:_____

_____
_____
_____

Wine: _____Year:_____
Notes:_____

_____
_____
_____

Wine: _____Year:_____
Notes:_____

_____
_____
_____

Wine: _____Year:_____
Notes:_____

_____
_____
_____

Drytown Cellars
Open daily 11am - 5pm.

>16030 Highway 49
>Drytown CA 95699
>209-245-350 866
>www.DrytownCellars.com

Drytown seems like an ironic name for a winery. But the winery takes its name from it's location just outside of Drytown, an old Gold Rush town. The town itself is worth a stop and a walk around with your camera or a sketchbook. Drytown Cellars is located on a portion of what used to be the Vaira Ranch, an early Amador County settlement.

Drytown Cellars, is another more recent winery, established in 2000. But they have made great progress and are producing some good, often award winning, wines. Their reputation is for "big" Zinfandels and wines with bold intense flavors and refreshing, fruitful whites.

Try their 2010 Amador County Sauvignon Blanc and their non-vintage Red-on-Red, a wonderful table wine.

Tasting Notes:

Wine: _____Year:_____
Notes:_____
_____
_____
_____

Wine: _____Year:_____
Notes:_____
_____
_____
_____

Wine: _____Year:_____
Notes:_____
_____
_____
_____

Wine: _____Year:_____
Notes:_____
_____
_____
_____

Wine: _____Year:_____
Notes:_____
_____
_____
_____

Nua Dair

Open Saturday & Sunday 10:30am - 5:30pm. Call for weekday appt.

> 13825 Willow Creek Road (Off the Jackson Highway)
> Ione CA 95649
> 209-245-5567
> www.nuadair.net

Nua Dair means "New Oak". The winery was previously named the Argonaut Winery. Their wines are available only in their tasting room. One of the more remote wineries in the book, the tasting room is out on Willow Creek Road in Ione.

They offer a wide range of wine varietals, including The ubiquitous Zinfandel, Sauvignon Blanc, Barbera, and Syrah. They also make what they call a Cal-Italia blend of Sangiovese and Cabernet Sauvignon called Banais.   They both grow their own grapes and buy grapes from other producers. The owner/wine maker, Mark McMaster is often in the tasting room and happy to answer questions about the wines and winery.

Tasting Notes:

Wine: _____Year:_____
Notes:_____
_____
_____
_____

Wine: _____Year:_____
Notes:_____
_____
_____
_____

Wine: _____Year:_____
Notes:_____
_____
_____
_____

Wine: _____Year:_____
Notes:_____
_____
_____
_____

Wine: _____Year:_____
Notes:_____
_____
_____
_____

The Sera Fina Cellars building is spacious and inviting.

Sera Fina Cellars

Open Saturday – Sunday 10am - 5:30pm
Monday – Friday by appointment only.

> 17000 Latrobe Road
> Plymouth California 95669
> 209-245-4300
> www.serafinacellars.com

Don't let my uninspired photograph of the winery fool you, Sera Fina Cellars is a wonderful place. The owner / wine maker, Paul Scotto is one to watch. He is a 5th generation wine maker. He's young and just getting started in his winemaking career. His wines are already good. I think he'll be able to make some really great wines in the future.

Sera Fina has become a must make stop when we go up to Amador County. Several of their wines have become house hold staples. Combine good wine, a friendly and engaging tasting room staff and an interesting building, and this wine drinker and architect is very happy.

If you follow my driving directions to the Amador County wineries and you opt to turn left onto Old Sacramento Road, you will miss Sera Fina Cellars. It's worth going crossing Old Sacramento Road and making the stop at Sera Fina then doubling back to Old Sacramento Road to make the turn to head toward Plymouth.

Their signature wine is the Dancing Grape, about which more in just a second. But, ask in the tasting room which of the young men is the original dancing grape and watch who blushes!

Tasting Notes

Sera Fina Cellars makes wine to be paired with food. All their wines are really "food friendly".

An Opinionated Guide to Gold Country Wines

They offer the Grand Daddy of the Amador County jug wines, a non-vintage sweet red wine called the Villa Armando California Vino Rustica Mello Red Wine. The name is as much a mouthful as the wine. It is sold in a one gallon jug – the biggest jug sold in Amador County. If you bring back a jug, they'll refill it for a lower purchase price.

The Sera Fina signature wine is probably their non-vintage Dancing Grape. It is a blend of Zinfandel, Barbera, Syrah and Cabernet Sauvignon. This is a wonderful wine to be paired with pastas in tomato sauces or with hamburgers, or even a good steak. It has become a household favorite. My partner likes a glass of the Dancing Grape at the end of a long day. But, who wouldn't?

I also like the 2009 Malvasia Bianca, a sweet white wine. The color is a clear, pale gold. It is a simple wine, with a strong taste of pears, peaches a granny smith apples on the front, a pleasant honey in the middle and a faint acid/gingery finish, that lasts quite a while. While sweet, is tart and dry enough to drink on it's own, and I think it would hold up well against a moderately spicy chicken or fish dish. But it would probably best be paired with fresh pears or peaches for desert. And frankly, on this sunny afternoon, it is really good all by itself.

Sera Fina Cellars also makes several flavored wine liquors, akin to port, but not. These are for those who like sweet flavored drinks for after dinner. I love the Chocolate Raspberry. A wine club member has made fudge with these liquors which are sinfully tasty.

Tasting Notes:

Wine: _____Year:_____
Notes:_____
_____
_____
_____

Wine: _____Year:_____
Notes:_____
_____
_____
_____

Wine: _____Year:_____
Notes:_____
_____
_____
_____

Wine: _____Year:_____
Notes:_____
_____
_____
_____

Wine: _____Year:_____
Notes:_____
_____
_____
_____

Sierra Ridge Winery

Open Friday - Sunday
11am - 4pm October - March
11am - 6:00 pm April - September

14110 Ridge Road
Sutter Creek CA 95685
209-267-1316
www.sierraridgewine.com

Sierra Ridge Winery, formerly known as Sutter Ridge is a fine small boutique winery established back in 1988. It is located not far from the Gold Rush town of Sutter Creek. The winery is situated up on a hill overlooking rolling vineyards.

All of their wines are hand crafted, and produced in small lots. They grow over 20 grape varieties including some more unusual varietals like Aglianico, Canaiolo Nero, Fresia, Vranac and Pinotage in addition to the Gold Country standards.

They produce small lots of single varietal wines as well as some really interesting blends. They are worth the drive!

Tasting Notes:

Wine: _____ Year:_____
Notes:_____

_____

_____

_____

Wine: _____ Year:_____
Notes:_____

_____

_____

_____

Wine: _____ Year:_____
Notes:_____

_____

_____

_____

Wine: _____ Year:_____
Notes:_____

_____

_____

_____

Wine: _____ Year:_____
Notes:_____

_____

_____

_____

Tanis Vineyards
Saturday and Sunday 10am - 5:30pm

13120 Willow Creek Road
Ione California 95640
209-274-4807
www.tanisvineyards.com

Located roughly half way between Drytown and Ione on Highway 124, Tanis Vineyards is one of the more remotely located wineries in the book. The other winery on Will Creek Road is Nua Dair.

Tanis is a very small winery making wines in small batches. The owners both tend the vines and make the wines themselves, ensuring that the wines represent their expression of the art of winemaking.

The grow and make the usual Amador County range of varietals: Viognier, Syrah, Primitivo, Zinfandel, Barbera. Tanis also makes less common Tempranillo and Pinotage varietals. Pinotage is more common in South Africa. Pinotage is typified by a deep red color, smokey, earthy flavors often with hints of banana.

Tasting Notes:

Wine: _____Year:_____

Notes:_____

_____

_____

_____

Wine: _____Year:_____

Notes:_____

_____

_____

_____

Wine: _____Year:_____

Notes:_____

_____

_____

_____

Wine: _____Year:_____

Notes:_____

_____

_____

_____

Wine: _____Year:_____

Notes:_____

_____

_____

_____

An Opinionated Guide to Gold Country Wines

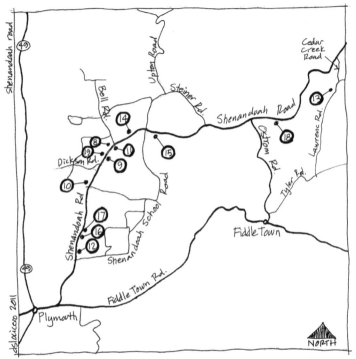

Map of Shenandoah Road wineries.

Shenandoah Road Wineries

Amador Cellars building is a simple "straw bale" barn nestled in the among the vines.

Amador Cellars

Open daily 11am - 5pm
     11093 Shenandoah Road
     Plymouth CA 95669
     209-245-6150
     www.amadorcellars.com

Amador Cellars is located in the heart of the Shenandoah Valley region of Amador County. Situated on a small hill, sheltered by several Valley Oak trees, they overlook the rolling vineyards. The building is a wonderful combination of traditional form and unconventional straw bale construction. The terrace is a wonderful place to sit down in the shade with a glass of wine and a friend.

The winery is at about the 1500 foot elevation and sits on granitic soil. All of their grapes are estate grown. They clearly take care growing of the grapes and making the wines. All the wines are aged for 8 to 20 months in oak barrels.

Amador Cellars is a family run winery. You will often find Larry Long, the owner/wine maker, his wife Linda, or other members of the family pouring wines in the tasting room. You are also likely to be greeted by Bailey and Kali, the winery dogs as you get out of your car. The atmosphere at the winery is friendly and informal.

Tasting Notes

But it is the wines we're most interested in. And Amador Cellars makes some really good ones. They are currently producing about 2200 cases of wine a year. They focus on the varietals that Amador's climate grows best: Zinfandels, Syrahs, Petite Syrahs and Barberas.

Their 2008 Barbera was the wine I started the tasting with. It has a lovely cocoa and raspberry nose. It is a lighter

An Opinionated Guide to Gold Country Wines

Barbera with nice plumy and strawberry notes balanced with vanilla and a hint of oak.

The next wine that I really liked was their 2007 Rocky Point Vineyard Zinfandel. This is an archetypal Amador Zin. This Zin is made from grapes grown in the vineyard you can see out the tasting room windows. Big, bold black cherry fruit on the first taste. This wine is down right jammy without being cloying or sweet. The tannins are soft, making this a good wine to drink by itself or with food.

The 2006 West Vineyard Zinfandel won an Amador County Fair Gold Medal. It is a nicely balanced wine with the taste of black cherry and currents. The wine maker's notes also mention pomegranate, but I wasn't getting it that day. The tannins and fruit a very nicely balanced. I can see why it's a medalist.

Amador Cellars also has a nice Zinfandel / Syrah blend. The 2008 is bottled in a jug and called Rapscallion. It is a spicy, drier wine with strong tannins and a black peppery taste. It would be ideal for a BBQ. It is 87.5% Zin and 12.5% Syrah.

Tasting Notes:

Wine: _____ Year:_____
Notes:_____
_____
_____
_____

Wine: _____ Year:_____
Notes:_____
_____
_____
_____

Wine: _____ Year:_____
Notes:_____
_____
_____
_____

Wine: _____ Year:_____
Notes:_____
_____
_____
_____

Wine: _____ Year:_____
Notes:_____
_____
_____
_____

Andis Wines production, storage and tasting facilities are all under one roof in a striking modern building.

Andis Wines

Open Friday - Monday 11am - 4:30pm and by appt.
    11000 Shenandoah Road
    Plymouth California 95669
    209-245-6177
    www.andiswines.com

One of the newer wineries in Amador County, Andis Wines has a lot going for it. As an architect, I stopped for the building, and ended up staying…and coming back…for the wines. Housed with all their facilities under one very stylish roof, the winery stretches across the top of a ridge with 270 degree views of the Shenandoah Valley. The building is uncompromisingly modern and comfortable, a stylish back drop for the serious and seriously fun subject of wine. And for those who prefer it, they also offer Laugunitas Ale on tap.

The owner, Andrew Friedlander has assembled a great crew for his winery. Not the least of which is the wine maker Mark McKenna. Mr. McKenna is a wine making genius. But more about that momentarily.

Andis Wines is one of the Amador County wineries that has a refillable bottle. The offer a one liter bottle, with an old fashioned stopper, that you can buy filled up with whatever wine they are featuring on tap, a Syrah the day we made the purchase. The liter costs $22. When you bring the bottle back, they'll refill it with whatever wine they currently have on tap for only $18; a bargain, and an interesting way to taste different wines.

Tasting Notes

When I was last there I tasted a Semillon (white), a Rose, a Barbera, a Grenache, Painted Fields – a blend and a Cab Franc.

An Opinionated Guide to Gold Country Wines

In retrospect, the 2010 Semillon was so good that I was convinced I had to have purchased at least one bottle. Really, I went searching for a bottle of this wonderful white that tastes of pears and star fruit. It was so refreshing!

The 2010 Rose was also a wonderful wine, with strawberry and watermelon flavors. I did buy one of these. It is waiting for a warm evening. I'll know the evening when it happens!

The 2008 Grenache is a very good bottle of wine. This wine alone would put Andis Wines on my list of top wineries in California. The nose is floral and almost like a good perfume. And it has an Oh, so drinkable balance of fruit, mineral flavors and tannins.

It is the 2009 Reserve Cabernet Franc that for me marks Mr. McKenna as a wine making genius and Andis Wines as one of the best wineries in the state. This wine is a dark, ruby red, with a startlingly herbal nose. So many California wines are all fruit and flowers. Encountering an herbal scent is remarkable. The flavor itself is subtle and complex with stone fruit flavors, a strong mineral quality and medium tannins. The wine maker told me that this is one of the wines about which he is most proud. He has every reason to be! It is one of the best wines I have had in years, maybe a decade.

Tasting Notes:

Wine: _____Year:_____
Notes:_____
_____
_____
_____

Wine: _____Year:_____
Notes:_____
_____
_____
_____

Wine: _____Year:_____
Notes:_____
_____
_____
_____

Wine: _____Year:_____
Notes:_____
_____
_____
_____

Wine: _____Year:_____
Notes:_____
_____
_____
_____

Bantam Cellars
Open daily 11am - 4pm

10851 Shenandoah Road
Plymouth CA 95669
209-245-6677
www.BantamCellars.com

Bantam Cellars was named after the hens and roosters raised by the owners. The tasting room is in a barn like building with a deeply shaded front porch. The folks inside are friendly and this is a very nice anti-dote to the Napa-light experience at the Villa Toscano winery just up the road. At Bantam Cellars there are real people and real wines.

Making mostly Italian style wines, including the unusual for California white varietal Vermentino. The Vermentino makes a crisp, dry white wine. They also make a Viognier which is not as dry with typical Viognier nose and a very peachy finish. For reds, I like their Coop D'Ville, which is a very drinkable blend of Zinfandel, Primitivo and Syrah. They also make single varietal Zinfandels, Primitivos and Barberas.

Tasting Notes:

Wine: _____Year:_____
Notes:_____
_____
_____
_____

Wine: _____Year:_____
Notes:_____
_____
_____
_____

Wine: _____Year:_____
Notes:_____
_____
_____
_____

Wine: _____Year:_____
Notes:_____
_____
_____
_____

Wine: _____Year:_____
Notes:_____
_____
_____
_____

Borjon Winery
Open Friday - Sunday 11am - 4pm

11270 Shenandoah Road
Plymouth CA 95669
209-245-3087
www.borjonwinery.com

Borjon Winery is one of a very small group of wineries in California that are Mexican-American owned and operated. They are the only Mexican-American owned winery in Amador County. The winery does not grow it's own grapes, but instead chooses to buy grapes from vineyards producing fruit the wine maker feels is best for their wines.

The family also imports and wholesales tequila, which gives the tasting room a somewhat confusing atmosphere, especially as there are no tequilas available for tasting.

The winery has only been opened since 2009, but they have wines going back to the 2007 vintage. I've tasted all the wines they offer for tasting and this is a winery to watch. If you like drier reds, you may like their wines a lot.

Tasting Notes:

Wine: _____Year:_____
Notes:_____
_____
_____
_____

Wine: _____Year:_____
Notes:_____
_____
_____
_____

Wine: _____Year:_____
Notes:_____
_____
_____
_____

Wine: _____Year:_____
Notes:_____
_____
_____
_____

Wine: _____Year:_____
Notes:_____
_____
_____
_____

Bray Vineyards
Open Wednesday - Monday 10am – 5pm

10590 Shendandoah Road
Plymouth CA 95669
209-245-6023
 www.brayvineyards.com

Established in 1996, they opened their doors to the public in 2004. Bray is a small, family-run winery. They make wines from the 20 varieties of grapes they grow in their own vineyards including Zinfandel, Sangiovese, Barbera, Syrah, Cabernet Sauvignon. In addition to Italian and French varieties, they have also started growing Spanish varietals.

Their signature wine is a Zinfandel and Sangiovese blend called BrayZin Hussy Red. There is also the BrayZin Hussy Blonde, which is a blend of Viognier, Verdelho and Sauvignon Blanc. Many of their wines have won awards at the county fairs in Amador County, El Dorado County, and Yolo County, among other awards.

They also make olive oil from several different kinds of olives they grow on their property.

Tasting Notes:

Wine: _____ Year:_____
Notes:_____
_____
_____
_____

Wine: _____ Year:_____
Notes:_____
_____
_____
_____

Wine: _____ Year:_____
Notes:_____
_____
_____
_____

Wine: _____ Year:_____
Notes:_____
_____
_____
_____

Wine: _____ Year:_____
Notes:_____
_____
_____
_____

Il Gioiello Winery and Morse Wines

Open Saturday and Sunday 11am - 5pm

22355 Lawrence Road
Fiddletown CA 95699
209-245-3395
www.morsewines.com

Located on the border of Amador and El Dorado counties, the Il Gioiello Winery and Morse Wines are located at a higher elevation than most of the other Amador County wineries and vineyards. They have a Bocce court just outside the tasting room! Wine club members can reserve the court in advance.

The Il Gioiello label is used to market their Italian varietal wines. They make these wines from estate grown Aglianico, Barbera, Montepulciano and Sangiovese. The Morse label is use to market their French, Rhone varietal wines. The make these wines form estate grown Viognier, Grenache, Syrah, Mouvedre and Petite Sirah.

They have a third label, Paralax, for wines sold direct to restaurants.

Tasting Notes:

Wine: _____Year:_____

Notes:_____

_____

_____

_____

Wine: _____Year:_____

Notes:_____

_____

_____

_____

Wine: _____Year:_____

Notes:_____

_____

_____

_____

Wine: _____Year:_____

Notes:_____

_____

_____

_____

Wine: _____Year:_____

Notes:_____

_____

_____

_____

Helwig Vineyards and Winery
Open Thursday – Sunday 10:30am – 4:30pm

11555 Shenandoah Rd
Plymouth CA
209-245-5200
www.helwigwinery.com

Helwig Vineyards and Winery is a new addition to the
Amador County wine scene. They are so new, in fact, that
I have not had the opportunity to visit the winery or taste
any of their wines.   When I was driving around Amador
County, researching this book all I could do was gaze
longingly at their tasting room and picnic pavilion from
the road as they were built on a distant ridge.

According to their website they are now open for tastings,
though construction will not be complete until the end of
August 2011.

The buildings look beautiful and I have heard that the
architect for the Helwig's is the same as for Andis.   I am
eager as a wine enthusiast and an architect to visit Helwig
and see what they have to offer!

Tasting Notes:

Wine: _____Year:_____
Notes:_____
_____
_____
_____
_____

Wine: _____Year:_____
Notes:_____
_____
_____
_____
_____

Wine: _____Year:_____
Notes:_____
_____
_____
_____
_____

Wine: _____Year:_____
Notes:_____
_____
_____
_____
_____

Wine: _____Year:_____
Notes:_____
_____
_____
_____
_____

Karmere Vineyards and Winery is housed in a French style building with lofty ceilings.

Karmere Vineyards and Winery

Open daily 11am - 5pm
No Limo groups.

     11970 Shenandoah Road
     Plymouth CA 95669
     209-245-5000
     www.karmere.com

Karmere (pronounced Car-MARE) Vineyards and Winery is a family winery. The tasting room is located in a somewhat kitschy, to my mind, French-country style building. The tasting room is large and opens out on to a terrace and picnic area that overlooks the vineyards. The tasting room staff is friendly and knowledgeable.

Their labels have a unique graphic style featuring somewhat creepy looking paintings of women. But maybe that's just me. But the kitsch and creepy can be forgiven because their wines are outstanding. There are many Gold Country wineries that produce one or two good wines. But the wineries that have as consistently good wines straight through the tasting as Karmere are few are far between. Basically, any of the reds made here is good or great.

Karmere's vineyards are planted with Viognier, Barbera, Syrah, Zinfandel and Nebbiolo. The vineyards are sustainably farmed. All of the wines and the vineyards are named after women who are members of the family.

Tasting Notes

They produce wines both single varietal wines as well as some interesting blends.

Karemare produces another of the Amador jug wines. Theirs is a non-vintage blend of Syrah, Petite Sirah, Zinfandel and Primitivo with the tongue twisting name Temperance Tarts Naughty Bawdy. The story behind the name is that the land where the winery is located was previously owned by a family that supported the temperance movement. The name is Karemare's way of celebrating the change. It is a very tasty and creamy table red tasting of plums and cherries that pairs well with spicy foods.

One of the interesting blends is their 2008 Empress Juana Primabera, a 50-50 blend of Primitivo and Barbera. This wine has a lovely color and smells of blackberries and cherry liquor. It tastes of blackberries, cherries, cocoa and vanilla with a lush mouth feel.

My favorite of their Syrah's is their 2007 La Petite Rachel Syrah. It has a spicy flavor with tasting of cassis and smoke. There is some oak in there too. It has a fair amount of tannin, but not overwhelming.

The Barbera is an award winner. They've won gold medals in Barbera competitions in Italy. The 2008 Empress Julie Ann Barbera is the most recent released vintage of Barbera. It's a super plumy wine with a faint cocoa flavor and caramel to finish.

Tasting Notes:

Wine: _____Year:_____
Notes:_____
_____
_____
_____

Wine: _____Year:_____
Notes:_____
_____
_____
_____

Wine: _____Year:_____
Notes:_____
_____
_____
_____

Wine: _____Year:_____
Notes:_____
_____
_____
_____

Wine: _____Year:_____
Notes:_____
_____
_____
_____

Nine Gables Vineyard

Open Thursday - Sunday 11am - 5pm,
Open Mondays 11am - 4pm and by appointment.

10778 Shenandoah Road
Plymouth CA 95669
209-245-3949
www.9gables.com

There is something about Nine Gables that I really like. It isn't their tasting room so much, or their setting, and the tasting room folks are nice enough, but it isn't them per se. What I like is the wines. Nothing is really great, but there are enough goodies on their tasting menu to make a guy pretty happy.

I like their 2008 Verdelho, a bright white with a floral nose which smells of vanilla & honey and tastes of pears and peaches. They also make flavored sparkling wines. Ordinarily this is just a red flag for awfulness. But not here. I actually liked their Raspberry Champagne which is crisp and not too sweet.

Nine Gables has a petite tasting room. If you are traveling in a big group or a limo, call ahead.

116

Tasting Notes:

Wine: _____Year:_____
Notes:_____
_____
_____
_____

Wine: _____Year:_____
Notes:_____
_____
_____
_____

Wine: _____Year:_____
Notes:_____
_____
_____
_____

Wine: _____Year:_____
Notes:_____
_____
_____
_____

Wine: _____Year:_____
Notes:_____
_____
_____
_____

The Jeff Runquist facilities includes a broad wraparound porch and a sheltered terrace.

Jeff Runquist Wines

Open Friday - Sunday 11 am - 5 pm

10776 Shenandoah Rd
Plymouth CA 95669
209-245-6282
www.jeffrunquistwines.com

Jeff Runquist Wines is a winery. They do not grow their own grapes. They purchase their fruit from some of the best vineyards in the state. Because Jeff Runquist buys grapes from all over the state, not all of the wines are "Gold Country wines" by my definition.

If you are new to Gold Country wines, this is a good place to stop and taste. Not only are the wines very good, but it will give you an opportunity to taste wines from various wine producing regions of Northern California and compare the qualities of Napa wines vs. those from Paso Robles and Amador County. Of course all of the wines are produced by a single wine maker and therefore do have similar qualities.

They have a reputation among the local's for making amazing wines. I've also been told that they are a little snobby. That has not been my experience, however. There is a slight whiff of Napa-tude about their website and marketing. But, all is forgotten when I have a glass of their wine in my hand.

The winery and tasting room are housed a low slung farm building with a nice wraparound porch. There is a small terrace at the front of the building for outdoor tasting. Inside the tasting room there is a view from the tasting room into the winery through a window in the back wall.

Tasting Notes

The last time I was there, I tasted wines made from fruit grown in Napa, Clarksburg, Paso Robles and Lodi. It was

An Opinionated Guide to Gold Country Wines

like a wine circuit of Northern California. But, honestly, the best of the wines were made from grapes grown in Amador County.

It's funny what you'll write down in your tasting journal. For the Jeff Runquist 2009 Primitivo, made from Amador County grown grapes, I wrote, "I want a car this color". It is a glorious cherry red. This wine tastes of cherries and Blackberry, with mild tannins and a minerality.

Jeff Runquist's 2009 "R" Zinfandel stood out in my mind not because of the aroma, which was indistinct to me that day, but because of the flavors of chocolate and berries. This wine has more pronounced tannins than the Primitivo and will, I think, age better. Not that it will survive for long in my cellar.

The other wine that I especially liked is the 2009 Barbera made with fruit grown at the Cooper Vineyards. Barbera's are infamously difficult to turn into a varietal wine. Many wine makers in Gold Country are now doing it with varied success. This is one of the more successful ones. It has a medium body with a deep ruby color. Typical of Barbera there is a lot of acid meaning this wine demands to be paired with food, ideally an earthy rustic casserole or roasted meat.

Tasting Notes:

Wine: _____Year:_____
Notes:_____
_____
_____
_____

Wine: _____Year:_____
Notes:_____
_____
_____
_____

Wine: _____Year:_____
Notes:_____
_____
_____
_____

Wine: _____Year:_____
Notes:_____
_____
_____
_____

Wine: _____Year:_____
Notes:_____
_____
_____
_____

Sobon Estate
Open daily 9:30am - 5pm

14430 Shenandoah Road
Plymouth CA 95669
209-245-6554
www.sobonwine.com

Founded in 1856, this Registered Historic Landmark is among the oldest wineries in California. Originally the D'Agostini Winery, it was purchased in 1989 by the Sobon family and renamed the Sobon Estate. The Shenandoah Valley Museum of Early Agriculture and Winemaking is located on the site. There is a lovely picnic area available to visitors.

The estate boasts one of the oldest old growth Zinfandel vineyards in Gold Country. The Sobon family pioneered organic grape growing and the planting of Rhône varietals in the Sierra foothills.

They make wines in the iconic California style: Sobon wines are noted for their strong fruit flavors with low tannins.

Tasting Notes:

Wine: _____Year:_____

Notes:_____

_____

_____

_____

Wine: _____Year:_____

Notes:_____

_____

_____

_____

Wine: _____Year:_____

Notes:_____

_____

_____

_____

Wine: _____Year:_____

Notes:_____

_____

_____

_____

Wine: _____Year:_____

Notes:_____

_____

_____

_____

Vino Noceto

Open Monday – Friday Noon - 4pm; Saturday & Sunday
11am - 5pm. Groups of 8 or more, please make an appt.

> 11011 Shenandoah Rd.
> Plymouth CA 95669
> 209-245-6555
> www.noceto.com

Just when you think you'll scream if you have to face
another Zinfandel, along comes Vino Noceto, a family
winery that specializes in Sangiovese. These folks have an
absolute passion for Sangiovese and it shows in their
wines. The winery, established in 1987, also makes wines
from Moscato Bianco, Barbara, the ever present Zinfandel
and a very nice white from Vernaccia.

This winery seems to have an active events schedule and it
seems like every time we go up to Gold Country to taste,
they're having a release party. Their members are
enthusiastic and loyal.

The winery, located at the intersection of Shenandoah and
Dickson Roads, is styled as an agricultural building. They
have a picnic area for visitors as well as bocce ball courts.

Tasting Notes:

Wine: _____Year:_____
Notes:_____

_____

_____

_____

Wine: _____Year:_____
Notes:_____

_____

_____

_____

Wine: _____Year:_____
Notes:_____

_____

_____

_____

Wine: _____Year:_____
Notes:_____

_____

_____

_____

Wine: _____Year:_____
Notes:_____

_____

_____

_____

An Opinionated Guide to Gold Country Wines

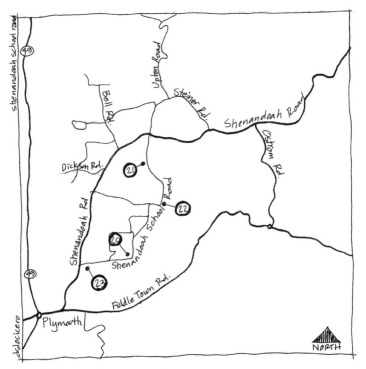

Map of Shenandoah School Road wineries.

Shenandoah School Road Wineries

C.G. DiArie Vineyard and Winery
Open Thursday - Monday 10am - 4:30pm

19919 Shenandoah School Rd
Plymouth CA 95669
209-245-4700
www.cgdiarie.com

C.G. DiArie is a family run winery established in 2000. They grow Zinfandel, Syrah, Petite Sirah, Primitivo, Cabernet Sauvignon and Cab Franc. Their vineyard also includes Amador County's "Grandpere Vineyard," which contains what are said to be the oldest Zinfandel vines in the U.S.

The C.G. DiArie tasting room has serene ambience. Don't miss the two art galleries that display a portion of the owners' collection of California art.

Vistors are welcome to picnic under the oaks or enjoy the Koi Pond and waterfall. There is a VIP tasting room available by appointment.

Tasting Notes:

Wine: _____Year:_____
Notes:_____
_____
_____
_____

Wine: _____Year:_____
Notes:_____
_____
_____
_____

Wine: _____Year:_____
Notes:_____
_____
_____
_____

Wine: _____Year:_____
Notes:_____
_____
_____
_____

Wine: _____Year:_____
Notes:_____
_____
_____
_____

Cooper Vineyards
Open Thursday - Monday 11am - 4:45pm

21365 Shenandoah School Road
Plymouth CA 95669
209-245-6181
www.cooperwines.com

Cooper Vineyards provides grapes to many of the local wineries. They also make their own wines. They are a small production facility, so their wines often sell out within six months or a year of release.

The tasting facility has a lovely shaded porch overlooking the grounds. The tasting room also has a huge roll up door that is usually open providing a spectacular view out over the vineyard.

Of their white's I liked their 2009 Roussanne which was light and spicy.

From their reds, the 2008 Sangiovese has a delicate nose of strawberry and vanilla. It tastes of cherry and cocoa. I've also tasted Cooper's 2008 Primitivo. It has raspberries on the nose and a spice and berries on the palate.

Tasting Notes:

Wine: _____Year:_____
Notes:_____
_____
_____
_____

Wine: _____Year:_____
Notes:_____
_____
_____
_____

Wine: _____Year:_____
Notes:_____
_____
_____
_____

Wine: _____Year:_____
Notes:_____
_____
_____
_____

Wine: _____Year:_____
Notes:_____
_____
_____
_____

Terra d'Oro
Open daily 10am - 4:30pm

20680 Shenandoah School Road
Plymouth CA 95669
209-245-6942
www.terradorowinery.com

Terra d'Oro, formerly known as Montevina Winery, was established in 1970 with some vineyards that date back to the 1880's. They released their first wines in 1973 making them the first vineyard in Amador County to make wine since the repeal of prohibition.

It is the largest winery in Amador County. The winery has a state-of-the-art production facility that produces some outstanding Zinfandels.

They also make wines from Moscato, Pinot Grigio, Barbera, Syrah and Sangiovese. They make a Nebbiolo Rose, a "Super Tuscan" blend and a Zinfandel Port. The Terra d'Oro white wines are made from fruit grown primarily in Santa Barbara, not true Gold Country wines.

Tasting Notes:

Wine: _____Year:_____
Notes:_____
_____
_____
_____

Wine: _____Year:_____
Notes:_____
_____
_____
_____

Wine: _____Year:_____
Notes:_____
_____
_____
_____

Wine: _____Year:_____
Notes:_____
_____
_____
_____

Wine: _____Year:_____
Notes:_____
_____
_____
_____

Wilderotter Vineyard and Winery
Open Friday - Monday 10:30am - 5pm

19890 Shenandoah School Road
Plymouth CA 95669
209-245-6016
www.WilderotterVineyard.com

Wilderotter Vineyard and Winery started out growing Zinfandel, Syrah, Barbara and Viognier grapes for sale to other wine makers. In 1999, they started making their own wines, with their first release in 2001. Now they produce about 3000 cases a year. Their tasting room, an elegant, Tuscan style building with shady patios and cooling fountains, was completed in 2004.

They now make wines not only from estate grown grapes but from fruit grown by other vineyards, not all of them Amador County. Check those labels, if you only want Gold Country wines!

Currently in addition to their first four varietals, they also make wines from Roussanne, Tempranillo, Petite Syrah, Mourvedre, Grenache and Sauvignon Blanc.

Tasting Notes:

Wine: _____ Year:_____
Notes:_____
_____
_____
_____

Wine: _____ Year:_____
Notes:_____
_____
_____
_____

Wine: _____ Year:_____
Notes:_____
_____
_____
_____

Wine: _____ Year:_____
Notes:_____
_____
_____
_____

Wine: _____ Year:_____
Notes:_____
_____
_____
_____

An Opinionated Guide to Gold Country Wines

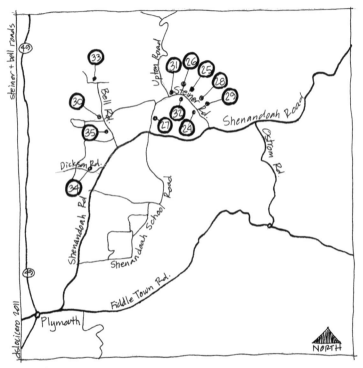

Map of Steiner and Bell Road wineries.

Steiner and Bell Roads Wineries

Amador Foothill Winery
Open Friday, Saturday, Sunday Noon - 5pm

12500 Steiner Road
Plymouth CA 95669
Tel: 209-245-6307
blog.amadorfoothill.com

Amador Foothill Winery is a small production winery, producing about 5,000 cases of wine a year. The owner-wine makers, Katie Quinn and Ben Zeitman handcraft their wines. They were pioneers of the single-vineyard zinfandel.

For white wines, they produce a popular Sauvignon Blanc and a late harvest Semillon. Amador Foothill Winery has been growing Semillon grapes for over 30 years. They also make a dry Rose.

In addition to their Zin's, the reds they make include a Tuscan-style Sangiovese, , a rare Italian varietal called Aglianico and a Rhone style blend of Grenache and Syrah called Katie's Cote.

Tasting Notes:

Wine: _____Year:_____
Notes:_____
_____
_____
_____

Wine: _____Year:_____
Notes:_____
_____
_____
_____

Wine: _____Year:_____
Notes:_____
_____
_____
_____

Wine: _____Year:_____
Notes:_____
_____
_____
_____

Wine: _____Year:_____
Notes:_____
_____
_____
_____

Charles Spinetta Winery and Wildlife Art Gallery

Open Saturday and Sunday 9am - 5pm
Open Monday, Thursday, and Friday 8am - 4pm

12557 Steiner Road
Plymouth CA 95669
209-245-3384
 www.charlesspinettawinery.com

The Charles Spinetta Winery and Wildlife Art Gallery is another of the Amador wineries that combines wine and art, in this case wildlife art.

The Spinetta family has farmed in Amador County since 1852. They grow and make wines from Barbera, Petite Sirah, Primitivo, Zinfandel, Chenin Blanc, Muscat and Tinta Madeira, as well as other rare, aged Amador County wines.

Their signature wine is probably their Heritage Red, which is an Italian style table red. They also make something called Frost Wine, which is made from Chenin Blanc grapes that have been frozen one the vine prior to picking.

Tasting Notes:

Wine: _____Year:_____

Notes:_____

_____

_____

_____

Wine: _____Year:_____

Notes:_____

_____

_____

_____

Wine: _____Year:_____

Notes:_____

_____

_____

_____

Wine: _____Year:_____

Notes:_____

_____

_____

_____

Wine: _____Year:_____

Notes:_____

_____

_____

_____

The grounds at Deaver Vineyards includes picnic tables on vast lawns arrayed at the edge of a small lake.

Deaver Vinyards

Open daily 10:30am - 5pm
12455 Steiner Road
Plymouth CA 95669
209-245-4099
www.deavervineyard.com

The Deaver Vineyards has become one of my favorite places in Amador County. They have a full calendar of events for their visitors and wine club members. Not only is the setting for the tasting room lush and beautiful, but the folks in the tasting room are friendly and extremely knowledgeable. This is a wonderful place to stop and have a picnic lunch on the lawn overlooking the small lake.

The Amador Harvest Inn, a Bed & Breakfast operated by the family, shares the grounds with the tasting room.

The Deaver family has been growing grapes in Amador since 1853, one of the oldest vineyards in Northern California. The age of the vines really makes a difference in the taste profile of the wines they make.

They produce a very broad selection of wines. They tasting room can't feature every wine produced. Sometimes you'll luck out and there will be something extra open. Be nice and they might offer you a taste.

Tasting Notes

The Deaver Vineyards page in my tasting journal is well worn and wine spotted: evidence of my appreciation for their wine maker's efforts.

I'm going to start off with their jug wine. Jug wines seem to be a trend right now in Amador County. But just because the wine comes in a jug doesn't mean that it isn't good. Theirs is called Deaver's Red Jug. It is a non-vintage table red. It is a little sweet and has a lower alcohol content. Table wines by definition have 12.5% alcohol or less. This is a great "go to" wine for casual parties or dinner with the family.

On a recent visit I tasted their 2007 Sierra Foothills Tempranillo. It is a light bodied red with a sharp, mineral quality. It tastes of cherry and leather in a good way. I find it a little high in acid for drinking on it's own. It would pair very well with food, including fish.

I also tasted and liked their 2007 Deaver Signature Zinfandel. In general their Signature wines are really good. But I find the scrawled labels, while stylish, difficult to read. This wine is smooth like silk. It is an arch-typical Amador Zin: bold fruit, soft tannins. This is a wine that would pair well with beef or even stews.

My personal favorite from Deaver Vineyards is the Ten Zin, in this case the 2007. Ten Zin is made from a blend of Zinfandel grapes from 9 different vineyard locations and a Primitivo. If the Signature Zinfandel is smooth like silk, this is smooth like velvet. It suits my palate perfectly, with a wonderful balance of fruit, acid, sweet and tannins.

Tasting Notes:

Wine: _____ Year:_____
Notes:_____
_____
_____
_____

Wine: _____ Year:_____
Notes:_____
_____
_____
_____

Wine: _____ Year:_____
Notes:_____
_____
_____
_____

Wine: _____ Year:_____
Notes:_____
_____
_____
_____

Wine: _____ Year:_____
Notes:_____
_____
_____
_____

Dillian Wines
Open Friday - Sunday 11am - 4:30pm

12138 Steiner Road
Plymouth CA 95669
209-245-3444
www.dillianwines.com

Dillian Wines is another small family winery with deep roots in Amador County. The family has opened the property since 1911. They specialize in Zinfandel, Primitivo, Barbera and Syrah. Tom Dillian worked at the historic D'Agostini winery. He has put that experience to good use at his own winery.

The tasting room is in a farm house style building with a wraparound porch that offers a shaded spot on a hot day. The tasting room itself is small, so if you're traveling in a big group be nice and call ahead.

Their wines are light to medium bodied and are high in acid. It means that they will pair well with foods, especially bar-b-que and stews. The best is their 2007 Tre Fratelli Zinfandel which has a smokey flavor and mineral quality.

Tasting Notes:

Wine: _____Year:_____

Notes:_____

_____

_____

_____

Wine: _____Year:_____

Notes:_____

_____

_____

_____

Wine: _____Year:_____

Notes:_____

_____

_____

_____

Wine: _____Year:_____

Notes:_____

_____

_____

_____

Wine: _____Year:_____

Notes:_____

_____

_____

_____

Dobra Zemlja

Open daily 10am - 5pm
12505 Steiner Road
Plymouth CA 95669
209-245-3183
www.dobraz.com

Dobra Zemly (pronounced dobra zem-ya) is Croatian for "Good Earth". The winery is housed in a restored 19th century farming facility and features a wine cave where the tasting room is located.

There is a long drive through the vineyards from the road back to the winery. The grounds are shady and overlook a small lake. Visitors are welcome to picnic in the designated picnic area. Even when it is busy, it is a tranquil location.

Dobra Zemlja specializes in Zinfandel, Syrah, Sangiovese, Barbera and Viognier. They are another of the Amador wineries that offer a jug wine. Theirs is a non-vintage blend of Zinfandel, Syrah and Sangiovese called Milan Ruz. Like Sera Fina, you can bring the jug back for a refill at a lower price than the initial purchase.

Tasting Notes:
Wine: _____ Year:_____
Notes:_____
_____
_____
_____

Wine: _____ Year:_____
Notes:_____
_____
_____
_____

Wine: _____ Year:_____
Notes:_____
_____
_____
_____

Wine: _____ Year:_____
Notes:_____
_____
_____
_____

Wine: _____ Year:_____
Notes:_____
_____
_____
_____

Driven Cellars

Open Thursday – Sunday 11am – 5pm. Limousines and buses by appointment only.

12595 Steiner Road
Plymouth, CA 95669
209-245-4545
www.drivencellars.com

Driven Cellars is, I think, the newest winery in the book. Although they planted their vineyards back in 1998, the winery itself has only just opened.

Located directly south of their neighbor Dobra Zemlja, they are approached up a gravel road that winds up to the top of a hill. The hill is crowned by a collection of rusted vehicles and farm equipment. The tasting room is tiny, but there is a picnic area behind the rusty vehicles with a beautiful view.

Their graphics are derived from the owner's interest in cars and motor racing. The labels are beautiful! When I was there, the place was packed with people and I was only able to taste a few of their wines. I think this is a winery to watch.

Tasting Notes:

Wine: _____Year:_____

Notes:_____

_____

_____

_____

Wine: _____Year:_____

Notes:_____

_____

_____

_____

Wine: _____Year:_____

Notes:_____

_____

_____

_____

Wine: _____Year:_____

Notes:_____

_____

_____

_____

Wine: _____Year:_____

Notes:_____

_____

_____

_____

Karly

Open daily 12 - 4pm except Thanksgiving, Christmas, New Years Day. Limousines by appointment only.

> 11076 Bell Road
> Plymouth CA 95669
> 209 245-3922
> www.karlywines.com

Karly Wines is located at the end of a long driveway that winds its way through the vineyards. The winery is most noted for its Zinfandels and Sauvignon Blanc's. But they also grow a Primitivo, Barbera, Vermentino, Sangiovese, Syrah, Petite Sirah, Mourvedre, Marsanne and, unusually, Granache Blanc. The winery now produces about 10,000 cases of wine every year. It is a friendly and unpretentious winery, quintessentially Gold Country in my opinion.

One of the grapes they grow, the Marsanne, is an unusual varietal for California. It is commonly grown in the Northern Rhone region of France. It is a low acid wine with flavors of peach, lichee, nuts and citrus. It takes to oak well and its golden color darkens as it ages. Worth a try, for sure!

Tasting Notes:

Wine: _____Year:_____
Notes:_____
_____
_____
_____

Wine: _____Year:_____
Notes:_____
_____
_____
_____

Wine: _____Year:_____
Notes:_____
_____
_____
_____

Wine: _____Year:_____
Notes:_____
_____
_____
_____

Wine: _____Year:_____
Notes:_____
_____
_____
_____

Renwood Winery
Open daily 10:30am - 5:30pm

12225 Steiner Road
Plymouth CA 95669
209-245-6979
www.renwood.com

The Renwood winery has a nice big tree in front of the building providing a nice place to sit down for a picnic lunch. There are several doors into the building and they all seem to lead to the same place, a large and loud tasting room. There is just a whiff of attitude here.

Robert Parker, the grand old man of wine criticism, has called Renwood a "tour de force" in winemaking. That may be his opinion, but I don't agree. Their wines are not bad, but nothing I tasted suited my palate. The wines I tasted seemed thin and highly acidic often with a bitter finish. But again, opinions differ Renwood is highly regarded and they have a very enthusiastic wine club.

Renwood has one of the so called "Grandpere" Vineyards, those oldest clones of Zinfandel dating back to the late 1800's.

Tasting Notes:

Wine: _____ Year:_____
Notes:_____

_____
_____
_____

Wine: _____ Year:_____
Notes:_____

_____
_____
_____

Wine: _____ Year:_____
Notes:_____

_____
_____
_____

Wine: _____ Year:_____
Notes:_____

_____
_____
_____

Wine: _____ Year:_____
Notes:_____

_____
_____
_____

Shenandoah Vineyards

Open daily 10am - 5pm

12300 Steiner Road
Plymouth CA 95669
209-245-4455
www.ShenandoahVineyards.com

Shenandoah Vineyards sits atop a hill overlooking the Shenandoah Valley. Go up the drive past a vineyard of old growth vines to a somewhat anonymous parking lot and enter the rustic tasting room and art gallery. Go. You'll like it.

The staff is completely unpretentious and friendly. The Shenandoah Vineyards were one of the first four modern wineries in Amador County. Established by the Sobon family in 1977, they now produce about 25,000 cases of wine a year.

The winery uses sustainable estate grown organic grapes to make all of their wines which are made and bottled on site. They make several award-winning wines.

Tasting Notes:

Wine: _____Year:_____
Notes:_____
_____
_____
_____

Wine: _____Year:_____
Notes:_____
_____
_____
_____

Wine: _____Year:_____
Notes:_____
_____
_____
_____

Wine: _____Year:_____
Notes:_____
_____
_____
_____

Wine: _____Year:_____
Notes:_____
_____
_____
_____

Storey Winery

Open Monday - Friday Noon - 4pm; Saturday & Sunday
11am - 5pm: Summer hours: Daily 11am – 5pm

> 10525 Bell Road
> Plymouth CA 95669
> 209-245-6208
> www.zin.com

Established in 1973, the Story Winery is a family-operated winery. The winery has a view of the Cosumnes River Canyon. They have vineyards that date back to the early 1900's. And they are quick off the mark with modern technology: they nabbed the coveted "zin.com" URL!

The specialties of the house are Mission and Zinfandel wines. You can't miss the 2007 Picnic Hill Zinfandel. If you are a Zin-ophile, you really can't miss a stop here.

There is a picnic area for visitors. One of the coolest things is if you don't want to be bothered to pack a picnic lunch, and you can plan ahead, you can pre-order a boxed lunch from them directly from their website no later than the Monday prior to your picnic. How cool is that?

Tasting Notes:

Wine: _____Year:_____

Notes:_____

_____

_____

_____

Wine: _____Year:_____

Notes:_____

_____

_____

_____

Wine: _____Year:_____

Notes:_____

_____

_____

_____

Wine: _____Year:_____

Notes:_____

_____

_____

_____

Wine: _____Year:_____

Notes:_____

_____

_____

_____

Terre Rouge and Easton Wines

Open Friday - Monday 11am - 4pm
September and October open 7 days a week 11am - 4 pm

10801 Dickson Road, just off Shenandoah Rd.
Plymouth, CA 95629-0041
209-245-4277
www.terrerougewines.com

One winery, two labels: Terre Rouge and Easton wines. The wine maker, Bill Easton, uses Terre Rouge for the Rhone varietal wines he makes and the Easton label for the non-Rhone varietal wines.

This winery makes artisan wines from Amador and other Sierra Foothills-region grapes. Jim Laube author of *California Wine*, named Terre Rouge/Easton his top-rated Sierra Foothill winery. Unlike my earlier difference of opinion with Robert Parker, I'm going to agree with Mr. Laube.

Wines here have a terrific balance of fruit, sweet, acid and tannins. Try the Terre Rouge Shenandoah Valley Viognier and any of the Easton Zinfandels. Oh, try 'em all!

Tasting Notes:

Wine: _____**Year:**_____
Notes:_____
_____
_____
_____

Wine: _____**Year:**_____
Notes:_____
_____
_____
_____

Wine: _____**Year:**_____
Notes:_____
_____
_____
_____

Wine: _____**Year:**_____
Notes:_____
_____
_____
_____

Wine: _____**Year:**_____
Notes:_____
_____
_____
_____

TKC Vineyards

Open Saturday 11am - 5pm; Sunday 1pm - 5pm; and by appointment

> 11001 Valley Drive
> Plymouth CA 95669
> 888-627-2356
> www.tkcvineyards.com

TKC Vineyards is something of an anomaly in the world of California wineries: they actually don't try to make wine from three dozen different varietals. Shocking, I know. They limit themselves to making small batches of Cabernet Sauvignon, Mourvedre and Zinfandel. And they do it very well.

TKC Vineyards was started by a rocket scientist and his wife in 1981. It remains a family affair. They don't grow their own grapes, but this leaves them free to buy the best available fruit from which to make their wines.

Their list of wines is short, but they are all good to terrific. Stop in and try their wines. The D.O.G. is a 60 – 40 blend of Cabernet Sauvignon and Mourvedre, aged 3-4 years in oak.

Tasting Notes:

Wine: _____Year:_____

Notes:_____

_____

_____

_____

Wine: _____Year:_____

Notes:_____

_____

_____

_____

Wine: _____Year:_____

Notes:_____

_____

_____

_____

Wine: _____Year:_____

Notes:_____

_____

_____

_____

Wine: _____Year:_____

Notes:_____

_____

_____

_____

An Opinionated Guide to Gold Country Wines

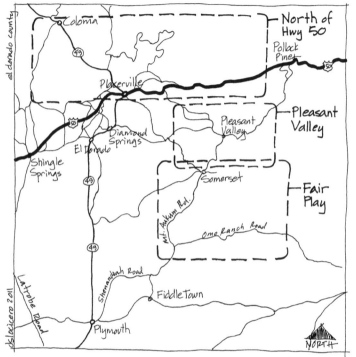

Map of El Dorado County showing groupings of wineries. See page 36 for a QR code that will link to the El Dorado Winery Association's map of member wineries.

See page 34 for a QR code that will take you directly to a Google Map of the Gold Country.

El Dorado County

For the purposes of this book, I have divided the wineries into three large groups which I am calling the North of Highway 50 group, the Pleasant Valley group and the Fair Play group.

The North of Highway 50 group is made up of wineries north of Highway 50. Two of these wineries are much further west than the others and will take longer to get to. (See map, page 166.)

The Pleasant Valley group is made up of wineries east of Placerville. (See map, page 166.)

The Fair Play Group is made up of wineries south of Placerville. (See map, page 168.)

An Opinionated Guide to Gold Country Wines

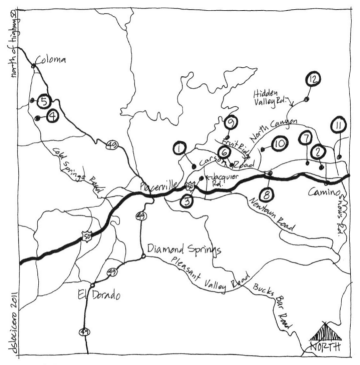

Map of the North of Highway 50 wineris.

In an effort to make your trip planning easier and help you eliminate doubling back and travelling the same roads forward and back, I have grouped the wineries in geographic areas. Refer to the maps for the most efficient driving. But for ease of reference, the winery descriptions themselves are arranged in the ever popular alphabetical order.

North of Highway 50

The wineries north of Highway 50 (see map, page 166) include the following:

1 Boeger
2 Crystal Basin
3 Fenton Herriott
4 David Girard – one of two furthest west
5 Gold Hill – one of two furthest west
6 Grace Patriot
7 Illuminare
8 Jodar
9 Lava Cap
10 Madrona
11 Para Vi
12 Wofford Acres

Pleasant Valley

The wineries the Pleasant Valley group (see map, page 168) include the following:

13 Auriga
14 Busby – in Somerset
15 Cantiga – in Somerset
16 Chateau Rodin
17 Holly's Hill
18 Miraflores
19 Narrow Gate
20 Sierra Vista

An Opinionated Guide to Gold Country Wines

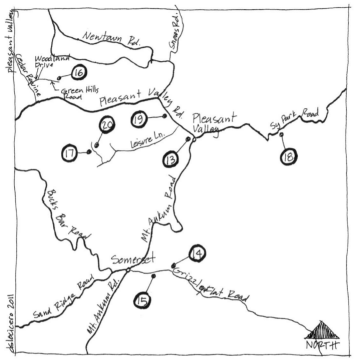

Map of the Pleasant Valley wineries.

Fair Play

The wineries in the Fair Play area (see map, page 168) include the following:

21 Cedarville – appointment required
22 Charles B. Mitchell
23 Colibri Ridge
24 Fitzpatrick
25 Granite Springs

26 Latcham
27 Perry Creek
28 Sierra Oak Estate
29 Single Leaf
30 Skinner
31 Oakstone
32 Windwalker
33 Mt. Aukum

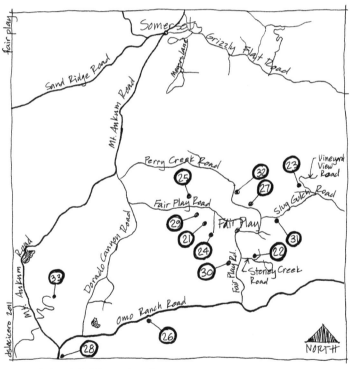

Map of the Fair Play wineries.

An Opinionated Guide to Gold Country Wines

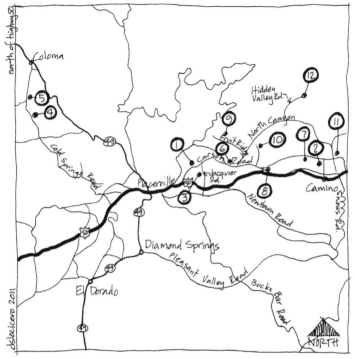

Map of wineries North of Highway 50.

Wineries North of Highway 50

Boeger Winery
Open daily 10am - 5pm

1709 Carson Rd.
Placerville, CA 95667
530-622-8094 or 800-655-2634
www.boegerwinery.com

The first El Dorado County vineyard to produce wine for sale after the repeal of prohibition, Boeger's vineyards were established in the 1860's. The Boeger family purchased the vineyard in 1972. They grow almost 40 different grape varietals and produce nearly 30,000 cases of wine a year.

The winery facility is large and extensive with a big tasting room set in grounds that include a lawn, stream, a patio and an historic wine cellar building that dates to 1872.

I'm not sure of the logic behind their different wine labels, but I tend to prefer the wines with the faux masking tape labels. These include a Primitivo, a Boejerlais, a Tempranillo and their Real Deal Red, a blend of Barbera, Grenache, Cabernet Sauvignon and Syrah.

Tasting Notes:

Wine: _____ Year:_____
Notes:_____
_____
_____
_____

Wine: _____ Year:_____
Notes:_____
_____
_____
_____

Wine: _____ Year:_____
Notes:_____
_____
_____
_____

Wine: _____ Year:_____
Notes:_____
_____
_____
_____

Wine: _____ Year:_____
Notes:_____
_____
_____
_____

Crystal Basin Cellars
Open daily 11am - 5pm

> 3550 Carson Road.
> Camino, CA 95709
> 530-647-1767
> www.crystalbasin.com

Crystal Basin Cellars, known as CBC, started out as a wine making cooperative composed of a circle of friends. Making wine together since 1988, they became a commercial operation in 2000. The folks at CBC are wine makers, not grape growers, and have been buying all of their fruit from the same vineyards for the past 15 years.

The tasting room is accessed of a small parking area located well off the road all the way up the drive. The tasting room is "intimate", by which I mean, tiny. The folks are really friendly, but if you're traveling in a group, even though CBC doesn't say it, call ahead.

CBC has a "minimalist" wine making style producing fruit forward wines using Zinfandel, Bordeaux and Rhône varietals. Their 2010 Cab Franc is a wonder of the wine maker's art.

Tasting Notes:

Wine: _____Year:_____
Notes:_____
_____
_____
_____

Wine: _____Year:_____
Notes:_____
_____
_____
_____

Wine: _____Year:_____
Notes:_____
_____
_____
_____

Wine: _____Year:_____
Notes:_____
_____
_____
_____

Wine: _____Year:_____
Notes:_____
_____
_____
_____

Fenton Herriott

Open daily 11am – 5pm

120 Jacquier Ct.
Placerville, CA 95667
530-642-2021
www.fentonherriott.com

Another of the younger wineries, Fenton Herriott began making wine in 2003. It is a family owned and operated outfit. The winery is located just down the road from the historic Smith Flat House which dates from the 1850's, now restored and home to an alternative health care practice.

Fenton Herriott makes wines from Chardonnay, Gewurztraminer, Sangiovese, Barbera, Merlot, Syrah, Cabernet Sauvignon, Zinfandel and Petit Sirah. In addition to growing their own grapes, the also buy fruit from other vineyards in El Dorado County. Their wines are complex and full bodied.

They have a picnic area and a large gazebo where you can enjoy a glass of wine and marvel at the views.

Tasting Notes:

Wine: _____Year:_____
Notes:_____
_____
_____
_____

Wine: _____Year:_____
Notes:_____
_____
_____
_____

Wine: _____Year:_____
Notes:_____
_____
_____
_____

Wine: _____Year:_____
Notes:_____
_____
_____
_____

Wine: _____Year:_____
Notes:_____
_____
_____
_____

David Girard Vineyards
Open daily 11am - 5pm

> 741 Cold Springs Rd.
> Placerville, CA 95667
> 530-295-1833
> www.dgvwines.com

David Girard Vineyards is situated in a little hollow just off the road and over the hill. They have 40 acres of vineyards growing Rhone varietals: Syrah, Grenache, Roussanne and Viognier. Almost all of the 5,000 cases of wine produced each year are estate grown. They also sell some of their grapes to other wineries.

The winery sits on a portion of the 160 acres that Albert Mosely claimed in 1849. Unlike other 49er's, he mined the pockets of the miners, opening a hotel and stage stop, the Bay State House.

The winery is also located on the site of the Wakamatsu Tea and Silk Colony which is recognized as the first Japanese settlement in the United States. A small group of Japanese immigrants lived on the site from 1869 to 1871.

Tasting Notes:

Wine: _____Year:_____

Notes:_____

_____

_____

_____

Wine: _____Year:_____

Notes:_____

_____

_____

_____

Wine: _____Year:_____

Notes:_____

_____

_____

_____

Wine: _____Year:_____

Notes:_____

_____

_____

_____

Wine: _____Year:_____

Notes:_____

_____

_____

_____

An early spring view from the terrace at Gold Hill Vineyard.

Gold Hill Vineyard
Open Thursday – Sunday 10am - 5pm

> 5660 Vineyard Lane
> Placerville, CA 95667
> 530-626-6522
> www.goldhillvineyard.com

Gold Hill Vineyards, on this site since the 1980's, is one of my favorite wineries in El Dorado County. The winery is situated on a hill overlooking a portion of their 50 acres of vineyards. They produce about 2500 cases of wine a year.

The tasting room is sunny and bright with a wrap around deck that looks out over a portion of the vineyards. The view is nice, and they do host weddings, but, man, it is their wines that bring me back again and again.

They have a passel of awards and it is easy to see why. The wine maker knows how to make the grapes sing. Gold Hill specializes in Bordeaux varietals, Chardonnay, Northern Rhone varietals and Barbera.

If you are traveling with a non-wine drinker, first, why? and second, Gold Hill also brews six different artisanal ales that should please them.

The folks here are serious wine makers, but they aren't pretentious at all. Down to earth and friendly, you'll feel right at home almost as soon as you've arrived.

Tasting Notes

Let's start with the "NV California Champagne". The French may get their knickers in a twist when we call our sparkling wines "champagne", but Gold Hill's product is worthy of the name. It is made with a combination of Chardonnay and French Colombard. It is a smooth champagne with very delicate bubbles. Not too dry, nor too sweet, we will pop open a bottle for special occasions, but often just to drink on a hot afternoon, or with a meal.

An Opinionated Guide to Gold Country Wines

Ever since the movie *Sideways* came out, Merlots have been much maligned. Their very drinkability seems to be held against them. They aren't "complex" enough. But Gold Hill's 2006 Merlot is one Merlot that has big bold flavors with the subtle complexities that make me think of Cabernet's. It is a complex wine, with hints of vanilla and cedar on the nose, but with dark, black cherry and plum flavors.

I can't not mention the 2007 Merititious, a scrumptious Bordeaux blend of equal parts of Cab Franc, Cabernet Sauvignon and Merlot grapes. It tastes of black cherry and a bit of oak, with moderate tannins. This is a wine I'd put down in my cellar for 5 or 10 years.

Tasting Notes:

Wine: _____Year:_____
Notes:_____
_____
_____
_____

Wine: _____Year:_____
Notes:_____
_____
_____
_____

Wine: _____Year:_____
Notes:_____
_____
_____
_____

Wine: _____Year:_____
Notes:_____
_____
_____
_____

Wine: _____Year:_____
Notes:_____
_____
_____
_____

Grace Patriot Wines
Open Thursday – Sunday 11am - 5pm

2701 Carson Road
Placerville, CA 95667
530-642-8424
www.gracepatriotwines.com

Grace Patriot Wine's new tasting room had not opened prior to my finishing the manuscript for this book. The new tasting room is surrounded by Grace Patriot estate vineyards and is located next to the Irving Ranch House and barn. The Irving Ranch House dates back to 1885. They have been making wines since 2004.

Tyler Grace, the wine maker at Grace Patriot, is a fellow Duck (University of Oregon graduate), so he's gotta be good, right? Well, Duck background or not, he is good. The wines made here are big, bold wines, dark in color and exceedingly well structured. They should age well, if you can keep from uncorking them.

They make Cabernet Sauvignon, Syrah, Tempranillo, Pinot Gris and a couple of super blends.

Tasting Notes:

Wine: _____Year:_____

Notes:_____

_____

_____

_____

Wine: _____Year:_____

Notes:_____

_____

_____

_____

Wine: _____Year:_____

Notes:_____

_____

_____

_____

Wine: _____Year:_____

Notes:_____

_____

_____

_____

Wine: _____Year:_____

Notes:_____

_____

_____

_____

Illuminare Winery

Open Friday – Sunday 11am - 5pm or by appt.

3500 Carson Road
Camino, CA 95709
530-647-1884
www.illuminarewinery.com

The tasting room for Illuminare Winery is located in the Camino Wine Plaza Building, which it shares with three other small wineries. The owners relocated to Gold Country from Alaska specifically to start a winery. They buy their grapes from various vineyards from the area.

Illuminare makes small lots of highly extracted wines, resulting in intensely flavored wines. They currently have Chardonnay, Cabernet Sauvignon, Mourvedre, Sangiovese, Zinfandel, Pinotage, Syrah and Barbera as well as a couple of bends, including their non-vintage Seeing Red and their vintage Momentum.

The folks at Illuminare will make you feel at home in the tasting room. They are excited and passionate about their wines and that can be tasted in their wines.

Tasting Notes:

Wine: _____Year:_____
Notes:_____
_____
_____
_____

Wine: _____Year:_____
Notes:_____
_____
_____
_____

Wine: _____Year:_____
Notes:_____
_____
_____
_____

Wine: _____Year:_____
Notes:_____
_____
_____
_____

Wine: _____Year:_____
Notes:_____
_____
_____
_____

A relaxing place to take a break from the hustle and bustle of everyday life. Even better with some wine.

Jodar Vineyards & Winery

Open daily 11am - 5pm Limos and buses by appointment.

3405 Carson Court
Camino, CA 95667
530-644-3474
www.jodarwinery.com

Jodar Vineyards and Winery tasting room is located in Camino, just east of Placerville, in the center of Apple Hill. Their terraced vineyards, literally blasted into the hillside, are located at some distance away. They're first vines were planted in 1986. They produced their first wines back in 1990. Jodar produces about 5,000 cases of wine annually.

The old tasting room was located at the vineyard and winery, but was relocated to the current location in 2005. The folks in the tasting room are very knowledgeable. Vaughn Jodar is often there himself. On weekends, they will offer food pairings to go with the wines. This gives you a better sense of how the wines can be paired and enhances the tasting experience.

They grow and make wines from Cabernet Sauvignon, Cabernet Franc, Merlot, Chardonnay, Zinfandel, Barbera and Sangiovese. Their winemaking style is bold fruit in balance with firm acid and oak, with moderate tannins.

As an architect who appreciates good design, I think that the Jodar wine labels are the best examples of label design in Gold Country. Tall and narrow on a black and grey striped back ground, the red outlined yellow script stands out as a graphic element and is legible and striking. Now, back to wine.

Tasting Notes

I am a member of the Jodar wine club and enjoy pretty much every wine they make.

An Opinionated Guide to Gold Country Wines

Let me start by saying that the Jodar table wine, a non-vintage called Vinosaurus Rex Red, is a blend of Zinfandel and Barbera. It is one of our house reds here at home. It pairs well with a multitude of foods and is an ideal wine for parties or BBQ's.

Their 2007 Sangiovese is the best made in El Dorado County, and possibly in all of Gold Country. It is cherry red in color with strawberry on the nose. It tastes of strawberry and pomegranate, with hints of vanilla and nutmeg.

Jodar's 2006 Cabernet Sauvignon smells of black cherry and plums. It tastes of black cherry with spices like clove. Personally I think it's over oaked, but it sells well.

Jodar is one of the wineries that has mastered the art of making an outstanding Barbera, Jodar's 2008 Barbera is my standard for Gold Country Barbera's. It is, as they call it, a cherry bomb of a Barbera. Intense red color with hints of blue, the color is mesmerizing. Nothing but cherry and black cherry on the nose. There is a strong cherry flavor with a nice vanilla and spice finish.

The vintage Black Bear Port is very popular. It pairs well with cherries and chocolate, but I find it just a little too sweet for my palate.

Tasting Notes:
Wine: _____Year:_____
Notes:_____
_____
_____
_____

Wine: _____Year:_____
Notes:_____
_____
_____
_____

Wine: _____Year:_____
Notes:_____
_____
_____
_____

Wine: _____Year:_____
Notes:_____
_____
_____
_____

Wine: _____Year:_____
Notes:_____
_____
_____
_____

Lava Cap Winery
Open daily 11am - 5pm

2221 Fruitridge Rd.
Placerville, CA 95667
530-621-0175
www.lavacap.com

Lava Cap Winery, so named because it sits on property characterized by volcanic soil. This is what happens when a wine maker had a previous life as a geologist. The owners purchased the property in 1981. Their first vintage was in 1986.

The tasting room is large and comfortable, complete with an expansive deck overlooking a picnic area, the vineyards and mountains in the distance. In addition to tasting wines, the facility also has a deli which sells light picnic food for purchase. Who needs to pack a lunch?

The wine making style here is well-balanced, full bodied wines with a strong fruit forward taste at the front, crisp acidity and soft tannins.

Tasting Notes:

Wine: _____Year:_____
Notes:_____
_____
_____
_____

Wine: _____Year:_____
Notes:_____
_____
_____
_____

Wine: _____Year:_____
Notes:_____
_____
_____
_____

Wine: _____Year:_____
Notes:_____
_____
_____
_____

Wine: _____Year:_____
Notes:_____
_____
_____
_____

Madroña Vineyards
Open daily 11am - 5pm

> 2560 High Hill Rd.
> Camino, CA 95709
> 530-644-5948 or 800-230-7662
> www.MadronaVineyards.com

Madrona Vineyards is in the heart of the Apple Hill area. Getting to the tasting room takes some navigational skills as you turn off Carson Road onto High Hill, which feels a little like a parking lot because there is little or no distinction between road and parking for the buildings right at the turn. But it is worth working through the confusion.

The Madrona vineyards are planted with about 30 different Rhone and Bordeaux varietals. The major varietals are Zinfandel, Merlot, Syrah, Nebbiolo, Petit Verdot, Barbera, Roussanne, Viognier.

Their Chardonnay is one of the few Gold Country Chardonnays that I like. In fact, the white wines here are probably the best whites in Gold Country.

Tasting Notes:

Wine: _____Year:_____
Notes:_____
_____
_____
_____

Wine: _____Year:_____
Notes:_____
_____
_____
_____

Wine: _____Year:_____
Notes:_____
_____
_____
_____

Wine: _____Year:_____
Notes:_____
_____
_____
_____

Wine: _____Year:_____
Notes:_____
_____
_____
_____

ParaVi Vineyards
Open daily 11am – 5pm

2875 Larsen Drive.
Camino, CA 95709
530-647-9463
www.ParaVi.com

Perhaps the only Gold Country winery that only makes red wines, ParaVi Vineyards has embraced the truth of the Gold Country *terroir* and climate: reds are great here, whites are okay to good. Go with the strength of the *terroir*!

ParaVi is located in the Apple Hill area of El Dorado County, north east of Placerville. They have two regulation bocce ball courts. You can reserve them in advance through their website.

They make small batches of premium red wines. They have a policy of not making more than 3,000 cases of wine a year, and only make wines from Zinfandel, Merlot, Cabernet Franc and Syrah. This kind of specialization is resulting in amazing rich and complex wines that are good value, though not inexpensive.

Tasting Notes:

Wine: _____Year:_____

Notes:_____

_____

_____

_____

Wine: _____Year:_____

Notes:_____

_____

_____

_____

Wine: _____Year:_____

Notes:_____

_____

_____

_____

Wine: _____Year:_____

Notes:_____

_____

_____

_____

Wine: _____Year:_____

Notes:_____

_____

_____

_____

Wofford Acres Vineyards

Open Thursday – Sunday 11am – 5pm except
September & October: Wednesday – Monday 11am -5pm

1900 Hidden Valley Lane
Camino, CA 95709
530-626-6858 or 888-928-9463
www.wavwines.com

Wofford Acres Vineyards is hard to find, but worth the effort. Hidden Valley Lane, as it turns out, is aptly named! One of the smallest producers in this book, they make about 1,200 cases of wine a year. They opened in 2003, though the wine maker has over 30 years of wine making experience. The winery has a picnic area with a wonderful view for which visitors are invited to use. The Woffords say, "Come for the wine and stay for the view!"

Of the wines, I recommend trying their 2009 LaMancha Estate, a really interesting blend of Petite Sirah, Nebbiolo, Cabernet Sauvignon and Gewürztraminer. Smelling of berries and spice, those carry over to the palate with the addition of chocolate, the wine is robust and flavorful.

Tasting Notes:

Wine: _____Year:_____

Notes:_____

_____

_____

_____

Wine: _____Year:_____

Notes:_____

_____

_____

_____

Wine: _____Year:_____

Notes:_____

_____

_____

_____

Wine: _____Year:_____

Notes:_____

_____

_____

_____

Wine: _____Year:_____

Notes:_____

_____

_____

_____

An Opinionated Guide to Gold Country Wines

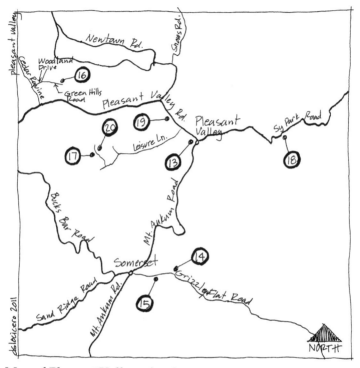

Map of Pleasant Valley wineries.

Pleasant Valley Wineries

Auriga Cellars

Open Friday – Sunday 11am - 5pm, or by appt.
4520 Pleasant Valley Road
Placerville, CA 95667
530-647-8078
www.aurigawines.com

Auriga Cellars takes its name from a Roman myth. Auriga was Zeus's nanny. When Zeus grew up he gave Auriga a magical horn that would grant it's possessor great abundance. This is also known as the Horn of Plenty.

Auriga wines are made from fruit grown locally in El Dorado County. They specialize in Syrahs and Zinfandels. Their vineyard is located outside of Placerville and is located on a warm southeastern slope with volcanic soils. They also have wines made from Barbera, Merlot, Cabernet Franc, Marsanne, Shiraz, and a Riesling. The earliest release they have available is 2006.

If you buy a bottle at the winery, and you're staying in Placerville, ask for a restaurant coupon. Both Café Luna and Tortilla Flats restaurants in Placerville will waive their corkage fees if you open your bottle for a meal in their restaurants.

Tasting Notes:

Wine: _____ Year:_____

Notes:_____

_____

_____

_____

Wine: _____ Year:_____

Notes:_____

_____

_____

_____

Wine: _____ Year:_____

Notes:_____

_____

_____

_____

Wine: _____ Year:_____

Notes:_____

_____

_____

_____

Wine: _____ Year:_____

Notes:_____

_____

_____

_____

Busby Cellars
Open Friday – Sunday 11am - 5:30pm

6375 Grizzly Flat Rd.
Fair Play, CA 95684
530-344-9119
www.busbycellars.com

Busby Cellars is a small, family owned and operated winery. They only produce about 2000 cases a year. The winery sits on a portion of what used to be the historic Meyer Ranch and includes an old barn where miners used to stop and change horses on the way to Placerville from Lake Tahoe.

Busby Cellars has a fairly limited production including Zinfanels, Barberas, Syrahs and Viogniers. They make a blend called Meyers Ranch Red which is a blend of Petite Sirah, Syrah and Zinfandel. It's a pleasant table wine and at a bargain price. Seriously, if you like Busby's wines, the prices are insanely low.

The tasting room is at the top of a hill with panoramic views of their vineyards. There is a "winery dog" who will greet you. Hank is a friendly pup.

Tasting Notes:

Wine: _____Year:_____
Notes:_____
_____
_____
_____

Wine: _____Year:_____
Notes:_____
_____
_____
_____

Wine: _____Year:_____
Notes:_____
_____
_____
_____

Wine: _____Year:_____
Notes:_____
_____
_____
_____

Wine: _____Year:_____
Notes:_____
_____
_____
_____

Cantiga Wineworks

Open Friday – Sunday 11am - 5pm. Call ahead for an appointment for groups of 8 or more.

> 5980 Meyers Lane
> Fair Play, CA 95684
> 530-621-1696
> www.cantigawine.com

Cantiga Wineworks is located just east of Somerset. They have adopted a Gothic theme for their tasting room and graphics, which seems a little strange in Gold Country. But it works for them. The tasting room has a view of their estate vineyards.

They embrace what I call a "minimalist" approach to wine making. They rely on hand selecting the best fruit available and let the grapes natural characteristics come through with minimal manipulation by the wine maker. They avoid malolactic fermentation as much as possible. Unlike many Gold Country vintners, they actually make Chardonnay and have quite a few on the wine list.

Cantiga Wineworks make classic wines that go well with food and will cellar well.

Tasting Notes:
Wine: _____Year:_____
Notes:_____
_____
_____
_____

Wine: _____Year:_____
Notes:_____
_____
_____
_____

Wine: _____Year:_____
Notes:_____
_____
_____
_____

Wine: _____Year:_____
Notes:_____
_____
_____
_____

Wine: _____Year:_____
Notes:_____
_____
_____
_____

Chateau Rodin

Open Wednesday – Sunday 11am - 5pm

4771 Green Hills Rd.
Placerville, CA 95667
530-622-6839
www.chateaurodin.com

The Chateau Rodin released their first wines, a Chardonnay and a Zinfandel, in 1981. They have deep experience making growing grapes at this altitude and in his climate. That vast experience shows in their wines.

The wines produce here are aromatic and very fruit forward wines frequently spicy. Unlike other Gold Country wineries, Chateau Rodin doesn't try to grow every grape varietal that may thrive in the climate. They are focused on producing first quality Chardonnay, Zinfandel, Cabernet Sauvignon, Barbera, and Merlot. All of their wines are made from estate grown grapes.

The tasting room is intimate with a spectacular view of the Sierras.

Tasting Notes:
Wine: _____Year:_____
Notes:_____
_____
_____
_____

Wine: _____Year:_____
Notes:_____
_____
_____
_____

Wine: _____Year:_____
Notes:_____
_____
_____
_____

Wine: _____Year:_____
Notes:_____
_____
_____
_____

Wine: _____Year:_____
Notes:_____
_____
_____
_____

Holly's Hill Vineyards
Open daily 10am - 5pm

> 3680 Leisure Lane
> Placerville, CA 95667
> 530-344-0227
> www.hollyshill.com

I like Holly's Hill Vineyards. I've been a member of their wine club. The tasting room sits up atop a small mountain, with a view southward over the vineyards.

They specialize in making wines from Rhone varietals. They grow Grenache Blanc, Roussanne, Viognier, Counoise, Grenache, Mourvedre, Petite Sirah, and Syrah.

Pardon me while gush about a wine which is sold out: the 2009 Counoise. This wine is a light red, with strawberries and cherries on the nose, and tasting of cherries, honey and pepper. As it breaths, it takes on a creamy mouth feel. It's one of the best light red's I've ever had. I also really like their Viognier, a drier version of this wine, which has a peachy start with citrus and an almost apricot finish. And don't miss their Patriarche, a classic Rhone blend.

Tasting Notes:

Wine: _____Year:_____
Notes:_____
_____
_____
_____

Wine: _____Year:_____
Notes:_____
_____
_____
_____

Wine: _____Year:_____
Notes:_____
_____
_____
_____

Wine: _____Year:_____
Notes:_____
_____
_____
_____

Wine: _____Year:_____
Notes:_____
_____
_____
_____

Close up view of the tower at the tasting building at Miraflores Winery. The beams in the tasting room are from the old Embarcadero building in Oakland, California.

Miraflores Winery
Open daily 10am - 5pm

2120 Four Springs Trail
Placerville, CA 95667
530-647-8505
www.mirafloreswinery.com

If their wines weren't so good, the growing Napa Valley quality of this winery would be annoying. They seem to be modeling themselves on the ways of Napa and Sonoma valley wineries. I encourage them not to move in that direction.

Look past the foofy Napa style though, and taste their wines. They are making some of the best wines in El Dorado County at the moment. These are highly structured wines typified by strong tannins that soften over time. Great wines to cellar!

The winery is situated in a lovely canyon, with the production building at the bottom of the hill and their new tasting room up at the top. The massive beams of the tasting room were salvaged from the old Oakland Ferry Building that was torn down in 1939.

They pride themselves on doing things the old fashioned way, including foot stomping! That makes me laugh. I just can't get that episode of *I Love Lucy* out of my head. All of the labor intensive efforts pay off.

Tasting Notes

Their 2007 Herbert Vineyard Zinfandel is my current favorite at Miraflores. This is a wine that really needs to be paired with a serious beef roast or other hearty meat dish. I taste blackberry and black cherry with a peppery finish. The tannins are strong, and I trust they'll soften over time.

An Opinionated Guide to Gold Country Wines

The 2005 Petite Sirah smells like blackberry jam. That is carried through on the palate with strong berry flavors. When I tasted it they had it paired with salty French fries with a garlic aioli. It seemed an odd pairing to me, but the wine was a strong and refreshing counter to the salty garlicky goodness.

If they have any left by the time this book goes to print, try the 2005 Methode Ancienne. This is one of the wines that Marco Cappelli, the wine maker, has been crafted using the oldest and simplest wine making methods, including foot-stomping the grapes to extract the juices. The wine tastes of cherry and red currant with a whiff of violets. It is a wonderful wine to drink by itself or paired with a great beef stew.

Tasting Notes:

Wine: _____Year:_____
Notes:_____

_____
_____
_____

Wine: _____Year:_____
Notes:_____

_____
_____
_____

Wine: _____Year:_____
Notes:_____

_____
_____
_____

Wine: _____Year:_____
Notes:_____

_____
_____
_____

Wine: _____Year:_____
Notes:_____

_____
_____
_____

An Opinionated Guide to Gold Country Wines

Narrow Gate Vineyards

Open Friday – Saturday 10am - 5pm, Sunday Noon - 5 pm

4282 Pleasant Valley Rd.
Placerville, CA 95667
530-644-6201
www.narrowgatevineyards.com

Narrow Gate Vineyards is another of my favorite wineries. And, yes, my partner and I are members of their wine club.

Like most of the wineries in the Pleasant Valley region of El Dorado County, they grow Rhone varietals like Syrah, Cabernet Sauvignon, Cab Franc, Petite Syrah as well as Primitivo, and Viognier. All of their wines are made from estate grown grapes which are grown organically.

Frank and Teena are the owners and wine makers and you'll often meet them behind the bar in the tasting room as well. They make wine that tastes good. Does that sound strange or obvious? What I mean is that they aren't wed to the idea of making varietal wines. If it looks like the grapes need to be blended to bring polish or balance to a wine, that's what they do. So they blend most of their

217

wines. They realize that wine is a beverage, and they are out to make the best they can.

Tasting Notes

Frank crafts wines that seem to be tailored specifically for my palate, so selecting three wines to discuss here is a real dilemma.

After much deliberation, I'll start out by discussing the Narrow Gate 2009 Viognier Roussanne, Estate. It is a blend of 88% estate grown Viognier and 12% estate grown Roussanne. The Roussanne tempers the typical sweetness of the Viognier and makes for a beautifully balanced white wine.

I also really like the 2007 Estate Dunamis™, one of the best Rhone blends in Gold Country. It is a Chateau Neuf du Pape style blend of 58% Grenache, 33% Syrah and 9% Mourvedre. It is a big wine which has clove, smoke and leather on the nose all of which can be tasted along with berries and stone fruit. It has strong tannins and a long, lingering finish. This wine is simply outstanding.

Narrow Gate also prides itself on a remarkable chocolate flavored port. They are currently selling their 2009 Chocolate Splash, El Dorado. It is made from a blend of 6 different port varietals and infused with actual chocolate. This flavored port is something more than a gimmick. It is a tasty dessert wine that is popular with wine lovers and non wine drinkers alike.

Tasting Notes:

Wine: _____Year:_____
Notes:_____
_____
_____
_____

Wine: _____Year:_____
Notes:_____
_____
_____
_____

Wine: _____Year:_____
Notes:_____
_____
_____
_____

Wine: _____Year:_____
Notes:_____
_____
_____
_____

Wine: _____Year:_____
Notes:_____
_____
_____
_____

Sierra Vista Vineyards & Winery
Open daily 10am - 5pm

4560 Cabernet Way
Placerville, CA 95667
530-622 -7221 or 800-946-3916
www.sierravistawinery.com

Sierra Vista Vineyards and Winery is located at the top of a small mountain on the edge of the Pleasant Valley area with a breath taking view of the Sierras from the lawn. It is an ideal setting for wine tasting or a picnic. The tasting room is simple and the staff is friendly and know their stuff. The owners are sometimes in the tasting room pouring tastings, too.

John and Barbara MacCready have been making small lots of estate grown Rhône wines including Syrah, Viognier, Roussanne, Grenache, Mouvedre and Rhône blends as well as traditional wines since 1977.

Sierra Vista makes both an unoaked and an oaked Chardonnay. I recommend tasting both, side by side, so you can get an idea of what oak does to the flavor and mouth feel of a Chardonnay. Then taste some other wines.

Tasting Notes:

Wine: _____Year:_____

Notes:_____

_____

_____

_____

Wine: _____Year:_____

Notes:_____

_____

_____

_____

Wine: _____Year:_____

Notes:_____

_____

_____

_____

Wine: _____Year:_____

Notes:_____

_____

_____

_____

Wine: _____Year:_____

Notes:_____

_____

_____

_____

An Opinionated Guide to Gold Country Wines

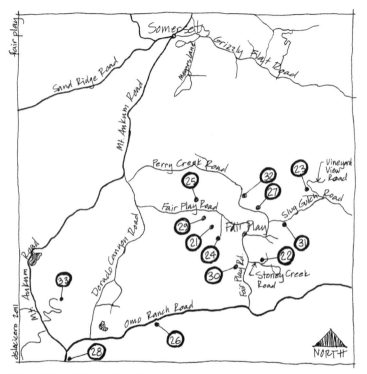

Map of Fair Play wineries.

Fair Play Wineries

Cedarville Vineyard & Winery

Tasting and tours by appointment only

6320 Marestail Rd
Fair Play, CA 95684
530-620-9463
info@cedarvillevineyard.com
www.cedarvillevineyard.com

Cedarville Vineyard and Winery is open only by appointment. You must call or email in advance to arrange a visit. I cannot speak with any authority on Cedarville Vineyard, as I regret that I was unable to visit the winery or tasted any of their wines prior to getting the book manuscript to the printer. I have spoken with several locals, however, who absolutely raved about how good the wines were here. You can bet that I will be visiting Cedarville soon. Check the companion website, OpinionatedWineGuide.com, for an update about Cedarville.

Cedarville's wines are produced solely from their estate grown grapes. They grow Zinfandel, Cabernet Sauvignon, and the Rhone Varietals Grenache, Viognier and Petite Sirah.

Tasting Notes:

Wine: _____ Year: _____
Notes: _____
_____
_____
_____

Wine: _____ Year: _____
Notes: _____
_____
_____
_____

Wine: _____ Year: _____
Notes: _____
_____
_____
_____

Wine: _____ Year: _____
Notes: _____
_____
_____
_____

Wine: _____ Year: _____
Notes: _____
_____
_____
_____

Colibri Ridge Winery & Vineyard
Open Friday – Sunday 11am - 5pm

6100 Gray Rock Rd.
Fair Play, CA 95684
530-620-7255
www.colibriridge.com

Colibri is Spanish for "hummingbird". It is also Italian for "snowcap". In this case, the owners are hummingbird enthusiasts as well as wine makers. The winery opened in 2004 and has been producing popular wines ever since. The tasting room is actually a corner of the barrel room inside the working winery. There is a picnic area just uphill from the tasting room among the granite outcroppings shaded by oak trees.

For such a young winery, they have an extensive list of wines from a long list of varietals. They make a Chardonnay and a Viognier. They also make A Petite Sirah, Mourvedre, Zinfandel, Syrah, Cabernet Sauvignon, Merlot, and some blends. Try the 2006 Beija Flor Tradicional, a port made from 4 different Portuguese varietals. Also try their 2006 El Dorado Rufous Red, a blend named after their winery dog.

Tasting Notes:

Wine: _____Year:_____
Notes:_____
_____
_____
_____

Wine: _____Year:_____
Notes:_____
_____
_____
_____

Wine: _____Year:_____
Notes:_____
_____
_____
_____

Wine: _____Year:_____
Notes:_____
_____
_____
_____

Wine: _____Year:_____
Notes:_____
_____
_____
_____

Fitzpatrick Winery & Lodge
Open Wednesday – Monday 1 am - 5pm

7740 Fairplay Rd.
Fair Play, CA 95684
530-620-3248 or 800-245-9166
www.fitzpatrickwinery.com

Fitzpatrick Winery & Lodge is the Fair Play region's oldest winery, having opened in 1980. The winery is housed in a massive log lodge, with spectacular, panoramic views and five B&B rooms. They offer a rustic Ploughman's Lunch on Saturday and Sunday between Noon and 4:30pm. On weekdays, you can put together a picnic from their Deli case.

The owners are dedicated to organic and sustainable farming practices and an overall eco-friendly approach to life and business. Their wines are made from CCOF certified organic estate grown grapes. They use solar-powered and bio-fuel driven eco-friendly techniques.

They make over 15 different wines. Did you know that not all wines can be considered Vegan? Fitzpatrick actually makes some Vegan wines.

Tasting Notes:

Wine: _____Year:_____

Notes:_____

_____

_____

_____

Wine: _____Year:_____

Notes:_____

_____

_____

_____

Wine: _____Year:_____

Notes:_____

_____

_____

_____

Wine: _____Year:_____

Notes:_____

_____

_____

_____

Wine: _____Year:_____

Notes:_____

_____

_____

_____

Granite Springs Winery

Open Saturday & Sunday 11am - 5pm

5050 Granite Springs Rd.
Fair Play, CA 95684
530-620-6395 or 800-638-6041
www.granitesprings.com

Granite Springs was purchased by Latcham Vineyards in 1994. Originally planted by Les Russell, Granite Springs' vines were planted in 1980. One of the oldest vineyards in the Fair Play region, the vineyard at Granite springs produces Zinfandel, Cabernet Franc, Petite Sirah, Syrah and Cabernet Sauvignon, Merlot and Sauvignon Blanc.

While the wines here are similar to those produced at Latcham Vineyards, Granite Springs has some nice wines of their own.

I'm especially fond of their 2006 Black Muscat, a fortified dessert wine made from the Muscat grape. It tastes strongly of blackberry and stone fruit, but without the thick, syrupy mouth feel one often gets from ports.

Tasting Notes:

Wine: _____Year:_____
Notes:_____
_____
_____
_____

Wine: _____Year:_____
Notes:_____
_____
_____
_____

Wine: _____Year:_____
Notes:_____
_____
_____
_____

Wine: _____Year:_____
Notes:_____
_____
_____
_____

Wine: _____Year:_____
Notes:_____
_____
_____
_____

The view from the small picnic area at Latcham Vineyards. It is a great place to pause and eat and take in the view.

Latcham Vineyards

Open Thursday – Monday 11 am - 5 pm, or by appt.

2860 Omo Ranch Rd.
Mt. Aukum, CA 95656
530-620-6642 or 800-750-5591
www.latcham.com

Latcham Vineyards is a family run vineyard and winery started by Frank Latcham back in 1981. They started making wine from their own grapes in 1990. They grow their own Chardonnay, Zinfandel, Cabernet Franc and Petite Sirah.

Located on the southern edge of the Fair Play region, and close to the Amador County line, the tasting room is located just off Omo Ranch Road in a rustic agricultural building. There is a nice lawn area with a view over the vineyards where visitors can picnic.

The Latcham wines have won hundreds of award, which are all on display in the tasting room. While their wines are well received by the critics, they haven't let it go to their heads. It is a friendly and down to earth atmosphere that greets visitors to their tasting room.

I recently had the good fortune to meet and chat with their wine maker, Ruggero Mastroserio. He is an artist with wine and a philosopher. Our conversation was focused on wine and started out simply with chat about the wines he was pouring but quickly became philosophical about wine making and even touched on the spirituality of wine!

Tasting Notes

There are so many wines to love here. I'll start with the Latcham Vineyards Gold Rush Red, a table wine. This is a wine that is full flavored and complex, but without the overwhelming attention seeking of a Zinfandel or Cabernet. When I first tasted it, I liked it and bought several bottles. It goes so well with food, I often wish I'd bought a case or two.

At the most recent Passport event, I did a vertical tasting of Latcham Vineyards Cab Francs, tasting a 2000, 2003, 2004 and 2007. The 2000 was clearly the best of the four. It was rich and subtle with hints of vanilla and cherry. I'm afraid to say, that I did not care for the 2004 which seemed to have a tobacco flavor I didn't like. But the 2007, though young, is a Cab Franc that will be on a par with the 2000 once it's has a few more years in the bottle.

Perhaps the best wine I've had in the last year, the 2008 Latcham Granite Petite Sirah, is an "ultra premium" European style wine hand crafted by Ruggero Mastroserio. It has a fruit on the nose and is smooth to drink with a unique and faintly licorice finish. The batches are small and the prices, therefore, big, but well worth every penny. I am not a Petite Sirah fan, but Mastroserio's artistry comes out in this wine and made me an enthusiastic fan of this wine.

Tasting Notes:

Wine: _____Year:_____
Notes:_____
_____
_____
_____

Wine: _____Year:_____
Notes:_____
_____
_____
_____

Wine: _____Year:_____
Notes:_____
_____
_____
_____

Wine: _____Year:_____
Notes:_____
_____
_____
_____

Wine: _____Year:_____
Notes:_____
_____
_____
_____

Charles B. Mitchell Vineyards
Open daily 11am - 5pm

8221 Stoney Creek Rd.
Fair Play, CA 95684
530-620-3467
www.charlesbmitchell.com

Charles B. Mitchell Vineyards is located in the heart of the Fair Play district. Their tasting room, attached to the winery, is a large room that feels to me like an old world wine cellar. The staff here is friendly and knowledgeable without any pretense. There is a picnic area complete with a bocce ball court.

They make wines from 30 different varietals and also import French sparkling wines. They both grow their own grapes and buy grapes from other vineyards, from Gold Country and from around Northern California.

The 2008 Estate Grand Reserve is a super smooth Bordeaux blend, and the most expensive wine on their current list. But they have a remarkable number of good wines for under $20/bottle.

Tasting Notes:

Wine: _____Year:_____

Notes:_____

_____

_____

_____

Wine: _____Year:_____

Notes:_____

_____

_____

_____

Wine: _____Year:_____

Notes:_____

_____

_____

_____

Wine: _____Year:_____

Notes:_____

_____

_____

_____

Wine: _____Year:_____

Notes:_____

_____

_____

_____

View of the pergola outside the tasting room at Mt. Aukum Winery. It is a great place to sit with a glass of wine and enjoy the awesome view.

Mount Aukum Winery

Open daily 11am - 5pm

6781 Tower Rd.,
Somerset, CA 95684
530-620-1675 or 800-591-WINE
www.mountaukum.com

Mount Aukum Winery is one of my favorite wineries. My partner and I are members of their wine club. They produce some of the biggest red wines around. Full bodied, bold and fruity wines with good tannins and structure enough to cellar for years, their wines seem tailor made for my palate.

Sitting atop a small mountain at the far south west end of El Dorado County, the drive up the mountain to the winery over a single lane winding road, feels treacherous, but the white knuckles and beads of perspiration are worth it for the view and the wines once you reach the winery.

Mt. Aukum specializes in Rhône and Bordeaux style wines. What that means here is big, bold reds. They grow Zinfandel, Petite Syrah, Petite Verdot and Cabernet Sauvignon. They also source Syrah, Malbec and Mouvedre from other local vineyards to use in their wines.

The wine maker, Michel Prod'hon, was born in France and has been involved in wine for most of his life. He is particularly drawn to the potential in Rhone and Italian varietals.

Tasting Notes

Michel Prod'hon doesn't make a bad wine. I am not quite as fond of the Mt. Aukum White's as I am of their Reds.

Since I have to limit myself to just a few wines, I will start with the 20067 BDX, a Bordeaux blend of 70% Cabernet,

An Opinionated Guide to Gold Country Wines

20% Merlot and 10% Cab Franc. It has a beautiful ruby color and has the big raspberry flavors, hints of spice and tannins of a Cabernet Sauvignon, but balanced with the smooth drinkability of the Merlot.

Another of my favorites is the 2007 Vertigo (Super Tuscan Blend) Fair Play. Featuring the Italian varietal Sangiovese (80%) blended with 10% Cabernet Sauvignon and 10% Cab Franc, it has medium tannins that are already starting to mellow. There are whispers of plum on the nose and nice red cherry flavors on the palate.

The 2007 Ace of Hearts is Mt. Aukum's port. Actually made from the Portuguese grapes Tinto Cao, Tempranillo, Tourgia and Souzao, this is about as authentic a Port as is made anywhere in the USA. It smells and tastes faintly of caramel and has a lovely velvety texture on the tongue.

Tasting Notes:

Wine: _____Year:_____
Notes:_____
_____
_____
_____

Wine: _____Year:_____
Notes:_____
_____
_____
_____

Wine: _____Year:_____
Notes:_____
_____
_____
_____

Wine: _____Year:_____
Notes:_____
_____
_____
_____

Wine: _____Year:_____
Notes:_____
_____
_____
_____

Oakstone Winery

Open Wednesday – Sunday 11am - 5pm, limousine groups and groups of 8 or more, please call for an appointment.

> 6440 Slug Gulch Rd.
> Fair Play, CA 95684
> 530-620-5303 or 877-OAK-STONE
> www.oakstone-winery.com

Oakstone Winery really is located on Slug Gulch Road. In Gold Country, gold sizes were categorized as dust flakes, nuggets and slugs. Slugs were the largest and most desirable. Today, the gold "slugs" are wine bottles.

Oakstone is one of the larger wine producers in El Dorado County, producing in excess of 10,000 cases of wine a year. They have even started a new label, Obscurity Cellars, to specialize in wines made from lesser known grape varietals.

Try their non vintage Slug Gulch Red, a blend of Zinfandel, Cabernet Sauvignon, Primitivo, Petite Sirah, Sangiovese and Merlot. It is robust and complex and worth a lot more than what they charge. Also try their 2008 Cabernet Sauvignon, a bold Cab with mild tannins.

Tasting Notes:

Wine: _____ Year:_____

Notes:_____

_____

_____

_____

Wine: _____ Year:_____

Notes:_____

_____

_____

_____

Wine: _____ Year:_____

Notes:_____

_____

_____

_____

Wine: _____ Year:_____

Notes:_____

_____

_____

_____

Wine: _____ Year:_____

Notes:_____

_____

_____

_____

Perry Creek Winery
Open daily 11am - 5pm

> 7400 Perry Creek Rd.
> Fair Play, CA 95684
> 530-620-5175 or 800-880-4026
> www.perrycreek.com

Perry Creek Winery is very popular. When I meet people who know about Gold Country wines, they generally mention Perry Creek as a place to try. Located in the Fair Play area, they have a lovely tasting room which also features a gourmet deli case so you can pull together a picnic lunch on the spot.

They say that they "strive for excellence by developing California flavors with European style". They grow and make wines from Zinfandel, Syrah, Petite Sirah, Barbera, Cabernet Sauvignon, Merlot, Chardonnay, Viognier and Muscat Canelli.

All 40 acres of their vineyards are sustainably farmed. They take a long view in their approach to grape growing and winemaking.

Tasting Notes:

Wine: _____Year:_____
Notes:_____
_____
_____
_____

Wine: _____Year:_____
Notes:_____
_____
_____
_____

Wine: _____Year:_____
Notes:_____
_____
_____
_____

Wine: _____Year:_____
Notes:_____
_____
_____
_____

Wine: _____Year:_____
Notes:_____
_____
_____
_____

Sierra Oaks Estates

Open Wednesday – Sunday 1 am - 5pm. Limousines and groups of 8 or more please call for an appointment.

> 8171 Mt. Aukum Rd., Suites 104-105
> Mt. Aukum, CA 95656
> 530-620-7079
> www.sierraoaksestates.com

Sierra Oaks Estates is a 40-acre vineyard and winery located in the Fair Play area. They have a very friendly tasting room that also features an art gallery that features local artists.

Another one of the few Gold Country wineries that is focusing solely on red wines made in small lots. They grow and produce wines from Merlot, Syrah, Zinfandel, Cabernet Sauvignon and Petite Sirah. Their blends also include Barbera and Cabernet Franc.

Try their 2005 El Dorado Cabernet Sauvignon. It is a big Cab that tastes of berries and a little bit of green olive. The tannins are not over powering and the finish just seems to linger like an afterglow.

Tasting Notes:

Wine: _____Year:_____
Notes:_____
_____
_____
_____

Wine: _____Year:_____
Notes:_____
_____
_____
_____

Wine: _____Year:_____
Notes:_____
_____
_____
_____

Wine: _____Year:_____
Notes:_____
_____
_____
_____

Wine: _____Year:_____
Notes:_____
_____
_____
_____

Single Leaf Vineyards and Winery
Open Wednesday – Sunday 11am - 5pm

7480 Fairplay Rd.
Fair Play, CA 95684
530-620-3545
www.singleleaf.com

Single Leaf Vineyards and Winery has been growing grapes since 1988 when they bought an existing Zinfanel vineyard in the Fair Play area. They opened their winery in 1993. Their approach to wine making starts in the vineyard, where they maintain low yield crops. With fewer grapes on the vines, the grapes have more intense flavors, and that translates into the wines. They produce between 4,000 and 5,000 cases of wine each year.

Single Leaf grows and makes wines from Chardonnay, Cabernet Sauvignon, Barberas, Cabernet Franc, Malbec and Petite Sirah. But their reputation lies with their Zinfandels. They will make and bottle up to five different Zinfandels each year. Their practice of dry farming, not using irrigation, is one of the reasons their Zinfandels are so intensely flavored.

Tasting Notes:

Wine: _____Year:_____

Notes:_____

_____

_____

_____

Wine: _____Year:_____

Notes:_____

_____

_____

_____

Wine: _____Year:_____

Notes:_____

_____

_____

_____

Wine: _____Year:_____

Notes:_____

_____

_____

_____

Wine: _____Year:_____

Notes:_____

_____

_____

_____

Skinner Vineyards
Open Friday – Sunday 10am - 5pm

8054 Fair Play Rd.
Somerset, CA 95684
530- 620-2220
www.skinnervineyards.com

The Skinner family had deep roots in El Dorado County. The first Skinner, James, was a gold miner in 1852, who planted his first vineyard in 1860, and soon after started what is said to be the first commercial vineyard in America. While they are farming different land than the original Skinner, the current family takes great pride in their heritage.

They make wines from the same Rhone varietals that were planted by James back in the 19th century. They grow and make wines from Viognier, Roussanne, Marsanne, Syrah, Grenache, and Mourvedre.

Their new tasting room has just opened at press time and I have not yet had the opportunity to visit it or to taste their wines. You can bet that it's on my list of places to go for my very next expedition to Gold Country.

Tasting Notes:
Wine: _____Year:_____
Notes:_____
_____
_____
_____

Wine: _____Year:_____
Notes:_____
_____
_____
_____

Wine: _____Year:_____
Notes:_____
_____
_____
_____

Wine: _____Year:_____
Notes:_____
_____
_____
_____

Wine: _____Year:_____
Notes:_____
_____
_____
_____

Windwalker Vineyard

Open daily 11am - 5pm. Limousines and groups of 8 or more please call for an appointment.

>7360 Perry Creek Rd.
>Fair Play, CA 95684
>530-620-4054
>www.windwalkervineyard.com

The Windwalker Vineyards, said to be named after a race horse, started out over 30 years. The owners started out as home wine makers and graduated to the big leagues when they purchased their vineyard. The tasting room is congenial and they offer a picnic area for visitors.

They offer Sauvignon Blanc, Chardonnay, Viognier, Barbera, Cabernet Sauvignon, Cabernet Franc, Merlot, Petite Verdot, Sangiovese, Malbec, Primitivo, Syrah, Zinfandel and Muscat. They also make a couple of red blends.

Try their 2008 Malbec. Windwalker is one of only a very few Gold Country wineries attempting a Malbec and theirs is worth trying.

Tasting Notes:

Wine: _____ Year:_____
Notes:_____
_____
_____
_____

Wine: _____ Year:_____
Notes:_____
_____
_____
_____

Wine: _____ Year:_____
Notes:_____
_____
_____
_____

Wine: _____ Year:_____
Notes:_____
_____
_____
_____

Wine: _____ Year:_____
Notes:_____
_____
_____
_____

An Opinionated Guide to Gold Country Wines

List of Gold Country Wine Events

This is a list of the major Gold Country wine events other than the State Fairs. The list is by no means exhaustive, many wineries sponsor their own events by themselves or in concert with a small group of wineries. It is worth it to check the website of a winery to see what they might have planned before you head out. Sometimes it's nice to plan a wine tasting trip around an event.

January
Barrel Tasting Weekend
Check www.eldoradowines.org for participating wineries, specific dates and ticket information.

An Opinionated Guide to Gold Country Wines

March / April
Behind the Cellar Door
Amador County's wineries celebrate Zinfandels. This is Amador County's biggest wine event. Check www.amadorwines.com for specific dates and ticket information.

Passport Weekend
The main event for enthusiasts and fans of El Dorado County wines is the annual Passport Weekend. The weather is usually fine and approximately 24 wineries offer tastings and food pairings for a limited number of tasters. This is the event that originally brought me to Gold Country and it's a permanent fixture on my calendar. Check www.eldoradowines.org for participating wineries, specific dates and ticket information.

April
Apple Blossom Festival
El Dorado County isn't just known for the wines. It is also an apple growing region and the Apple Blossom Festival celebrates all things apple. Many local wineries join in on the fun. Check www.eldoradowines.org for specific dates and participating wineries.

May
Rocks & Rhones
Pleasant Valley wineries Holly's Hill, Narrow Gate, Miraflores and Sierra Vista feature their Rhone varietals wines in a weekend of wine, music and art. Check www.eldoradowines.org and/or the participating wineries' websites for specific dates and ticket information.

June
Amador County Barbera Festival
2011 saw the first ever fest of all things Barbera hosted at Cooper Vineyards. It was a huge success and may become an annual event. Check www.barberafestival.com for information about possible future event.

FairPlay Wine Festival
FairPlay area wineries celebrate their unique wines with a weekend of tasting and music. Check www.eldoradowines.org and/or the websites for the participating wineries for specific dates and ticket information.

August
Slug Fest
The wineries along Slug Gulch Road (yes, really) celebrate their wines one weekend each August. The participating wineries include Colibri Ridge, Oakstone, Obscurity Cellars and DKCellars. Check www.eldoradowines.org and/or the websites for the participating wineries for specific dates and ticket information.

October
The Big Crush
Amador County wineries celebrate the harvest and crush with a two day event. Check www.amadorwines.com for specific dates and ticket information.

An Opinionated Guide to Gold Country Wines

Index of Wineries

This is a complete list of wineries included in this book in the ever popular alphabetical order.

An Opinionated Guide to Gold Country Wines

Andis Wines   98
11000 Shenandoah Road
Plymouth California 95669
209-245-6177
www.andiswines.com

Auriga Cellars   202
4520 Pleasant Valley Road
Placerville, CA 95667
530-647-8078
www.aurigawines.com

Avio Vineyards and Winery   76
14520 Ridge Rd.
Sutter Creek CA 95685
209-267-1515
www.aviowine.com

Bantam Cellars   102
10851 Shenandoah Road
Plymouth CA 95669
209-245-6677
www.BantamCellars.com

Boeger Winery   172
1709 Carson Rd.
Placerville, CA 95667
530-622-8094 or 800-655-2634
www.boegerwinery.com

Borjon Winery   104
11270 Shenandoah Road
Plymouth CA 95669
209-245-3087
www.borjonwinery.com

Bray Vineyards   106
10590 Shendandoah Road
Plymouth CA 95669
209.245.6023
 www.brayvineyards.com

Busby Cellars   204
6375 Grizzly Flat Rd.
Fair Play, CA 95684
530-344-9119
www.busbycellars.com

Cantiga Wineworks   206
5980 Meyers Lane
Fair Play, CA 95684
530-621-1696
www.cantigawine.com

Cedarville Vineyard & Winery   224
6320 Marestail Rd
Fair Play, CA 95684
530-620-9463
www.cedarvillevineyard.com

Chateau Rodin   **208**
4771 Green Hills Rd.
Placerville, CA 95667
530-622-6839
www.chateaurodin.com

Colibri Ridge Winery & Vineyard   **226**
6100 Gray Rock Rd.
Fair Play, CA 95684
530-620-7255
www.colibriridge.com

Convergence Vineyards   **78**
14650 Hwy 124
Plymouth CA 95669
209-245-3600
 www.convergencevineyards.com

Cooper Vineyards   **130**
21365 Shenandoah School Road
Plymouth CA 95669
209-245-6181
 www.cooperwines.com

Crystal Basin Cellars   **174**
3550 Carson Road.
Camino, CA 95709
530-647-1767
www.crystalbasin.com

Deaver Vinyards   **142**
12455 Steiner Road
Plymouth CA 95669
209-245-4099
www.deavervineyard.com

C.G. DiArie Vineyard and Winery   **128**
19919 Shenandoah School Rd
Plymouth CA 95669
209-245-4700
www.cgdiarie.com

Dillian Wines   **146**
12138 Steiner Road
Plymouth CA 95669
209-245-3444
www.dillianwines.com

Dobra Zemlja   **148**
12505 Steiner Road
Plymouth CA 95669
209-245-3183
www.dobraz.com

Driven Cellars   **150**
12595 Steiner Road
Plymouth, CA 95669
209-245-4545
www.drivencellars.com

Drytown Cellars   80

16030 Highway 49
Drytown CA 95699
209-245-350 866
www.DrytownCellars.com

Fenton Herriott   176

120 Jacquier Ct.
Placerville, CA 95667
530-642-2021
www.fentonherriott.com

Fitzpatrick Winery & Lodge   228

7740 Fairplay Rd.
Fair Play, CA 95684
530-620-3248 or 800-245-9166
www.fitzpatrickwinery.com

Il Gioiello Winery and Morse Wines   108

22355 Lawrence Road
Fiddletown CA 95699
209-245-3395
www.morsewines.com

David Girard Vineyards   178

741 Cold Springs Rd.
Placerville, CA 95667
530-295-1833
www.davidgirardvineyards.com

Gold Hill Vineyard   **180**
5660 Vineyard Lane
Placerville, CA 95667
530-626-6522
www.goldhillvineyard.com

Grace Patriot Wines   **184**
2701 Carson Road
Placerville, CA 95667
530-642-8424
www.gracepatriotwines.com

Granite Springs Winery   **230**
5050 Granite Springs Rd.
Fair Play, CA 95684
530-620-6395 or 800-638-6041
www.granitesprings.com

Helwig Vineyards and Winery   **110**
11555 Shenandoah Rd
Plymouth CA
209-245-5200
www.helwigwinery.com

Holly's Hill Vineyards   **210**
3680 Leisure Lane
Placerville, CA 95667
530-344-0227
www.hollyshill.com

Illuminare Winery   186
3500 Carson Road
Camino, CA 95709
530-647-1884
www.illuminarewinery.com

Jodar Vineyards & Winery   188
3405 Carson Court
Camino, CA 95667
530-644-3474
www.jodarwinery.com

Karly   152
11076 Bell Road
Plymouth CA 95669
209-245-3922
www.karlywines.com

Karmere Vineyards and Winery   112
11970 Shenandoah Road
Plymouth CA 95669
209-245-5000
www.karmere.com

Latcham Vineyards   232
2860 Omo Ranch Rd. (P.O. Box 80)
Mt. Aukum, CA 95656
530-620-6642 or 800-750-5591
www.latcham.com

Lava Cap Winery   **192**
2221 Fruitridge Rd.
Placerville, CA 95667
530-621-0175
www.lavacap.com

Madroña Vineyards   **194**
2560 High Hill Rd.
Camino, CA 95709
530-644-5948 or 800-230-7662
www.MadronaVineyards.com

Miraflores Winery   **212**
2120 Four Springs Trail
Placerville, CA 95667
530-647-8505
www.mirafloreswinery.com

Charles B. Mitchell Vineyards   **236**
8221 Stoney Creek Rd.
Fair Play, CA 95684
530-620-3467
www.charlesbmitchell.com

Mount Aukum Winery   **238**
6781 Tower Rd.,
Somerset, CA 95684
530-620-1675 or 800-591-WINE
www.mountaukum.com

Narrow Gate Vineyards 217
4282 Pleasant Valley Rd.
Placerville, CA 95667
530-644-6201
www.narrowgatevineyards.com

Nine Gables Vineyard 116
10778 Shenandoah Road
Plymouth CA 95669
209-245-3949
www.9gables.com

Nua Dair 82
13825 Willow Creek Road (Off the Jackson Highway)
Ione CA 95649
209-245-5567
www.nuadair.net

Oakstone Winery 242
6440 Slug Gulch Rd.
Fair Play, CA 95684
530-620-5303 or 877-OAK-STONE
www.oakstone-winery.com

ParaVi Vineyards 196
2875 Larsen Drive.
Camino, CA 95709
530-647-9463
www.ParaVi.com

Perry Creek Winery   244
7400 Perry Creek Rd.
Fair Play, CA 95684
530-620-5175 or 800-880-4026
www.perrycreek.com

Renwood Winery   154
12225 Steiner Road
Plymouth CA 95669
209-245-6979
www.renwood.com

Jeff Runquist Wines   118
10776 Shenandoah Rd
Plymouth CA 95669
209-245-6282
www.jeffrunquistwines.com

Sera Fina Cellars   84
17000 Latrobe Road
Plymouth California 95669
209-245-4300
www.serafinacellars.com

Shenandoah Vineyards   156
12300 Steiner Road
Plymouth CA 95669
209-245-4455
www.ShenandoahVineyards.com

Sierra Oaks Estates   246
8171 Mt. Aukum Rd., Suites 104-105
Mt. Aukum, CA 95656
530-620-7079
www.sierraoaksestates.com

Sierra Ridge Winery   88
14110 Ridge Road
Sutter Creek CA 95685
209-267-1316
www.sierraridgewine.com

Sierra Vista Vineyards & Winery   220
4560 Cabernet Way
Placerville, CA 95667
530-622 -7221 or 800-946-3916
www.sierravistawinery.com

Single Leaf Vineyards and Winery   248
7480 Fairplay Rd.
Fair Play, CA 95684
530-620-3545
www.singleleaf.com

Skinner Vineyards   250
8054 Fair Play Rd.
Somerset, CA 95684
530-620-2220
www.skinnervineyards.com

Sobon Estate 122
14430 Shenandoah Road
Plymouth CA 95669
209-245-6554
www.sobonwine.com

Charles Spinetta Winery and Wildlife Art Gallery 140
12557 Steiner Road
Plymouth CA 95669
209-245-3384
 www.charlesspinettawinery.com

Storey Winery 158
10525 Bell Road
Plymouth CA 95669
209-245-6208
www.zin.com

Tanis Vineyards 90
13120 Willow Creek Road
Ione California 95640
209-274-4807
www.tanisvineyards.com

Terra d'Oro 132
20680 Shenandoah School Road
Plymouth CA 95669
209-245-6942
www.terradorowinery.com

Terre Rouge and Easton Wines   160
10801 Dickson Road, just off Shenandoah Rd.
Plymouth, CA 95629-0041
209-245-4277
 www.terrerougewines.com

TKC Vineyards   162
11001 Valley Drive
Plymouth CA 95669
888-627-2356
 www.tkcvineyards.com

Vino Noceto   124
11011 Shenandoah Rd.
Plymouth CA 95669
209-245-6555
www.noceto.com

Wilderotter Vineyard and Winery   134
19890 Shenandoah School Road
Plymouth CA 95669
209-245-6016
www.WilderotterVineyard.com

Windwalker Vineyard   152
7360 Perry Creek Rd.
Fair Play, CA 95684
530-620-4054
www.windwalkervineyard.com

Wofford Acres Vineyards   **198**

1900 Hidden Valley Lane
Camino, CA 95709
530-626-6858 or 888-928-9463
www.wavwines.com

An Opinionated Guide to Gold Country Wines

Resources

The following are some resources that you may find useful or interesting:

Costa, Eric J., *Gold and Wine: A History of Winemaking in El Dorado County, California*, 2010, The El Dorado Winery Association, Placerville, CA.

> This book is available in many of the wineries in El Dorado County. It provides background information about the history of El Dorado County and the history of winemaking. Lavishly illustrated.

An Opinionated Guide to Gold Country Wines

McKowen, Dahlynn & Ken, *The Wine-Oh! Guide to California's Sierra Foothills*, 2009, Wilderness Press, Berkeley, CA.

> This book is available in a few of the wineries in Amador and El Dorado County. It covers a much larger area than this book and only discusses the wineries, not the wines.

Phillips, Mark, *Swallow This: The Progressive Approach to Wine*, 2009, 20 Sips, LLC, Chicago, IL

> This book is an excellent introduction to wine tasting.

Viniferra: The World's Great Wine Grapes and Their Stories, 2008, Ghigo Press, Venice, CA

> This is a set of individual cards with lush photographs of 45 different grape varietals on one side and information about the grapes' origins, myths and stories associated with them as well as their basic taste characteristics. Both fun and useful!

About The Author

David Locicero is a wine enthusiast and architect who has been exploring the wines of Northern California for years. He and his partner have traveled the Gold Country's back roads seeking out the little known wineries that are producing some of the best California wines available. He lives in the San Francisco Bay area with his partner. When he isn't working, he is an accomplished home chef and enjoys frequent trips to the Gold Country to savor the wines and meet new friends. He can be reached at david@opinionatedwineguide.com.

The QR code above, when scanned with your smart phone's bar code scanner app, will provide a direct link to the companion website, OpinionatedWineGuide.com.

An Opinionated Guide to Gold Country Wines

Coming in November 2011

Urban Wines:
An Opinionated Guide to the Bay Area's Urban Wineries
By David S. Locicero

The San Francisco Bay Area is host to a multitude of urban wineries: wineries located right in San Francisco, Oakland, Alameda and other Bay Area cities.

Want to go wine tasting but you got up too late to drive to Gold Country and you can't face the traffic on Highway 29 going to Napa? Taste local!

Urban wineries buy their grapes from the best vineyards in Napa, Sonoma, Amador, El Dorado and other wine growing regions in Northern California, but they make and bottle their wines right here in Bay Area cities.

Urban Wines: An Opinionated Guide to the Bay Area's Urban Wineries will be the definitive guide to urban wineries and related tasting rooms.
- Winery descriptions
- Wine tasting notes
- Wine, Sake, Distilleries, Breweries
- Maps
- Public Transportation options

OpinionatedWineGuide.com

Made in the USA
Charleston, SC
28 June 2011